Mother in the Mother

Looking back, looking
forward – women's reflections
on maternal lineage

Pippa Grace

WOMANCRAFT PUBLISHING

Praise for
Mother in
the Mother

This book is a compelling archive for the complex and ambivalent experiences of motherhood. In holding all these "stories within stories", Pippa reveals all too often unseen and unspoken matrlineal memories and moments. In making space for the very personal she reminds the reader of the what is radically political - human connection. She demonstrates a profoundly generous metholodgy invaluable for anyone wanting to understand contemporary motherhood, memory, ethics and the power of storytelling.

Dr Alex Wardrop, daughter, writer, mama

This beautiful project came along at a timely moment, I had just returned back to work at the Arts Council after having my first child. Mother in the Mother by Pippa Grace is a thought provoking piece, relevant and resonant for every mother, but inspiring and moving for everyone.

Nema Hart, Relationship Manager at Arts Council England

Timely and necessary, Mother in the Mother is a thought-provoking and vital read. Highly recommended for anyone wishing to learn more about the value and importance of mothers.

Dr Teika Bellamy, Managing Director of Mother's Milk Books

'A fascinating and powerful exploration of motherhood across generations. I loved the personal stories, and the clear sense that the Mother in the Mother project was an enriching experience for all who took part.'

Emylia Hall, novelist and founder of Mothership Writers

Mother in the Mother is an important resource for understanding our maternal lineage, and illustrates the importance of women having thoughtful spaces such as the ones Pippa facilitated to explore their significance. What inspired me in reading these stories is how mothers manage, often with few resources, to surpass their own experiences of being mothered as they become mothers themselves. Mother in the Mother's unique focus on intergenerational relations between grandmothers, mothers and daughters situates these often neglected relationships in new ways. Pippa Grace has generously shared her insights from years of artistic practice with mothers which will be invaluable to all those who want to centre and deconstruct motherhood in their work.

Dr Maud Perrier, senior lecturer in Sociology, University of Bristol

Pippa Grace has created a healing space for women to reclaim their Motherlines. This collection of women's stories from a rich diversity of cultures and backgrounds illuminates the intimate details of women's mysteries – how the embodied experience of giving birth can transform a woman's sense of self and the sacred in her relationship to her mother, her child and her female body.

Grace is a midwife to women's souls, bringing to contemporary lives the ancient wisdom of the Triple Goddess – personified on earth as daughter-mother-grandmother. Mother in the Mother is a gift for those who are mothers and/or have mothers.

Naomi Ruth Lowinsky, author of *The Motherline: Every Woman's Journey to Find Her Female Roots*

Mother in the Mother is full of powerful words and powerful stories about a most powerful subject: our maternal heritage and relationships. The voices of the women, together with Pippa's insight, form a roadmap of wisdom to navigate the twists and turns of our own maternal journeys and to cross the bridge from daughter to mother with joy and strength.

Vanessa Olorenshaw, author of *Liberating Motherhood*

Through her groundbreaking book, Mother in the Mother, Pippa Grace harnesses the power of one of our oldest teaching tools and healing arts – storytelling – to illuminate the wisdom of the Motherline. With encouragement and care, Pippa offers an empowering path for our most important stories to be examined, shared, and healed.

Melia Keeton Digby, author of *The Heroines Club* and *The Hero's Heart*

This brave piece of work dares to shed light on one of our most intimate relationships, revealing the flaws, truths and hopes inherent in being a mother.

Alison Hitchcock, Managing Editor at The Word Factory and founder of From Me to You

Pippa has taken the most primal of relationships, mother daughter, and gracefully managed to raise awareness of how that experience continues, down the line as daughter becomes mother. I love the different stories from different women, the acceptance that the relationship between mother and daughter can be many things, but is a significant one. Raising awareness of how mother sits within us as we mother is such a welcome exploration, inviting women to parent with increased awareness and understanding, and compassion. I absolutely loved reading this book

Dominique Sakoilsky, family and relationship therapist, and author of *The Seven Secrets of a Joyful Birth*

Mother in the Mother is a beautiful book, born out of a long and careful process of enquiry, creativity, conversation, and most of all intelligent listening.

Creative practice and personal reflection run throughout, and I love how much the care taken by Pippa, and her truly collaborative approach has enabled so many women to tell their personal stories. These are "the unwritten stories' so important to us all and I think crucial for us to hear to help us understand our own often complex relationships.

They are intensely personal but also speak to us all – as the book says, "every new mother was once a women's new infant". There is joy and there is sadness but mostly there is hope and a growing understanding of what is to share lineage and be a part of something bigger and beyond our control.

Dr. Carolyn Hassan, founder and director of Knowle West Media Centre

Pippa Grace's anthology Mother in the Mother is a vital documentation of the mythical and yet very raw, real power and influence of the matrilineal relationship which is rarely given proper voice and space within our patriarchal culture - the mysteries, magic and maelstroms - you will find it all here.

Matilda Leyser, founder of Mothers Who Make

Mother in Mother is an essential collective reflection on the roles of mothers across times and cultures, an unveiling and revealing storytelling of women's linages as a way forward to heal our future.

Dyana Gravina, Procreate Project founder and creative director

Published by Womancraft Publishing, 2019
www.womancraftpublishing.com

ISBN 978-1-910559-47-5
Also available in ebook format: ISBN 978-1-910559-46-8

A version of the introduction was first published in The Mother magazine.

Mother in the Mother logo, icons and cover design by Bart Blazejewski
Back Cover and interior layout by Lucent Word.

Internal photographs kindly provided by Mother in the Mother contributors including:

Adela Maryam Miles
Alex Wardrop (© Ursula Schlatter)
Amy Sinclair
Anita Maccallum
Anna Lagerdahl
Becky Slater
Carley Oates
Chantelle Mortimer
Charlotte Brydon-Smith
Chloe Bodard-Williams
Ella Bissett MacEwen
Elsie Thorpe

Faith Kent
Gemma Sparkes
Harriet Symon
Jo Pillinger
Karni Arieli
Kate Turton
Kayleigh Hunt
Monira Ibrahim
Sophie Barker
Tamzen Deeley
Yasmeen Akhtar

Images of the exhibition opening on p2 © Number Nine Photography
and on p7 © Sidz Photography.

*For my mum
and my 'other mothers'
especially my Nan, Mary, Tamar and Yen*

Contents

A woman is born with all the eggs she will ever have. The egg that made you was an egg inside your mother when she was just a foetus inside your grandmother.

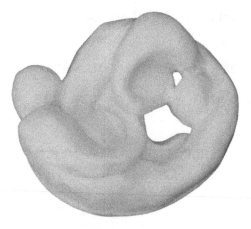

Project sculpture: *Three bodies*

Preface

Exploring maternal lineage

When a woman becomes a mother, it is often a time she reflects back upon the way she herself was mothered. Our maternal inheritance, from our mother, grandmother, great-grandmother and beyond, can have a great influence upon our lives and the ways in which we choose to bring up our own children.

Mother in the Mother explores this theme of maternal lineage through the stories of over fifty women. Each woman reflects on her journey into motherhood, alongside her relationship with her own mother and the relationships between herself, her mother and her children.

Mother in the Mother began its life in 2012 as a participatory arts project funded by Arts Council England and supported by Bristol-based arts organisation and charity, Knowle West Media Centre (KWMC). Over the next three years, more than two hundred women took part in the project, sharing their stories at creative workshops and celebratory events. Participants created chains of paper dolls, handmade books, and short films with their stories. These were displayed, alongside portrait photography and sculptures exploring maternal lineage, at public exhibitions held in Bristol and London in 2015-2016. Some women chose to write their stories, and this book shares some of those narratives.

In 2017 Arts Council England gave a further two years' funding to extend and develop the work begun in 'Mother in the Mother'. This enabled more workshops to take place and stories to be collected from a wider diversity of participants.

Between 2012 and 2018, 'Mother in the Mother' worked with a variety of women living in the UK, from a wide range of socio-economic and cultural backgrounds. These included, but were not restricted to: mothers in their teens, twenties, thirties, forties and fifties; pregnant women; grandmothers and great grandmothers; LGBT+ mothers; mothers of adopted or foster children; mothers who themselves were adopted; white, black, Asian and minority ethnic groups; mothers experiencing postnatal illness; mothers who were estranged from their own mothers; and mothers whose mums had died before they themselves had children. Workshops took place in Bristol, and the project received national press coverage on Woman's Hour, BBC Online, *The Mother* magazine and *Juno* magazine. On the back of this, stories were also collected online from a national, self-selecting group of mothers.

Exhibition opening at KWMC, Bristol, March 2015.

Foreword

by Naomi Stadlen

This anthology is an invitation for readers to reflect on the mothering we have each received. It's interesting for daughters who become mothers. Also fathers, uncles, aunts, cousins, and friends of families with children may find it revealing to think about how they themselves were mothered.

We all started our lives inside our mothers, and experienced from within the gamut of their moods. After our births, we learned to know them more consciously. Those of us who become mothers, as Pippa explains, usually think back to our own mothers. We ask ourselves whether we want to repeat what our mothers did, or do it differently. The mothers here show us how they made their choices.

This anthology shows several significant themes that may help readers with their own reflections. Mothers who valued their own mothers nearly always mention their protective strength as well as their love. Some describe what fun their mothers were, and the mischievous laughter they shared.

Mothers who had more problematic relationships rarely mention deliberate cruelty in this collection. What they describe is a *lack*. Daughters felt the lack deeply. A failure of the mother to hug is mentioned by several, and so are mothers who never told their daughters: "I love you." It sounds as if these simple, inexpensive demonstrations of motherly love make all the difference.

Some mothers can be unkind. My grandmother, a large woman, told my mother that she was 'too thin' to become a mother herself. My mother tried to be kinder to me, and I've tried to be kinder to my children than she was. At first, I was alarmed by Pippa's title, *Mother in the Mother*. I didn't want to think of my mother in me. But, like the other mothers here, I realise that mine developed a special strength of her own. That has given me something precious.

If we spend some time thinking about the influence of our mothers, we may avoid thoughtlessly repeating an unkind maternal pattern of relating to children. We may think of better ways to be. We may still repeat the unkind behaviour, and wish too late that we hadn't. But at least we can notice and be sorry. That's a step forward towards change.

Pippa sums up the strength of our 'maternal inheritance': "It is as if those links that connect us to our mother can never be fully severed; they run far deeper than our conscious selves…" So changing does not have to mean severing. Many mothers in this anthology show us how.

We can sift our inheritance. We can evolve with and beyond it.

Naomi Stadlen, 2019

Unpacking Matryoshka Dolls [1]

The story behind the stories

Mother to child and child to mother, this is the story that follows me, the ghost that haunts me. My daughter, my mother, her mother, her mother's mother. It is as if they have left footprints in the snow. Try as I might to deviate, my feet fall gently but firmly into their well-worn grooves. My daughter before me, my daughter after me. The times when I carry my daughter and the times when she carries me.

I am a mother to two daughters. My mother had three girls, of which I was the middle child. Her mother, my nan, had just one daughter. A propensity for having girls is not the only thing that travelled down our maternal line.

My nan had severe postnatal depression and spent six months of her infant's first year in a psychiatric ward. My mum had postnatal depression when I was born, and has said that she did not attach to me. I was lucky to escape postnatal depression after the birth of my girls; and our attachment felt solid from the start. But I did experience a huge amount of anxiety that affected the early months with my daughters.

I experienced the birth of my first daughter as deeply traumatic. We attempted a home birth but ended up in hospital. I was terrified and high on gas and air by the time we got there. As it came to the third stage I remember thinking: *there is no way I can get this baby out of my body.*

The midwife circumspectly switched off the gas and air, pulling me back into my body and my innate ability to birth. As my body opened to allow my daughter's passage into the world, I went from terror to a place of deep clarity. I had thought I was carrying a boy, but as soon as I heard her gender something slotted into place deep within me. I had a clear sensation of her going through labour in the future. Within this moment, this space outside of time, I realised that we were just tiny pinpoints along a long line of women, a maternal lineage stretching far away from us into the past and before us into the future.

When I later learnt that my daughter already possessed all the eggs she would ever have whilst she was in my womb, this deep link I felt between all of my maternal figures made perfect sense.

When I was a baby, my nan looked after me at times during my mother's postnatal depression and she was a close maternal figure in my life. My nan had a stroke when my eldest daughter was two. I had only very tentative contact with my birth family at this time, but over the next few weeks we all spent time in and out of hospital, living side by side in the waiting room. My nan never came out of hospital; she died a month later.

For that short space of time, in the way that hospitals can create a liminal space outside of everyday life, there we all were together: four generations of women from the same blood line. Our estranged maternal line was, for a while, intact. It was a powerful thing to experience, and went deeper than all the hurt and fracture: a time I will never forget.

The words at the top of this introduction came to me after my nan's death. And with them the seed of this project was born.

The Project

Mother in the Mother started its life around my kitchen table on Mother's Day 2012, nine months after the birth of my second daughter. In my practice as a socially engaged artist, I work with individuals and communities, supporting them to tell their stories creatively. Now, for the first time, I chose to work on a project that included my own story. I brought together a small group of women to talk about the reality of their journeys of motherhood in the context of their maternal lineage, over tea, coffee and a traditional Mothering Sunday simnel cake, rich with marzipan and currants. Something was liberated that day as we shared stories and dared to talk honestly about our experiences – the dark as well as the light.

I spoke for the first time about the insidious anxiety I had experienced after my first daughter was born; of how I continually 'saw' her body broken on the floor, how these images filled my waking hours. Other women shared similar stories. I wasn't alone, which was a very powerful and healing realisation.

This became the basis for a participatory arts project: creating a safe space for women to share the realities of their experiences, hearing and honouring them, and supporting mothers to create something with their stories. The overarching theme of maternal lineage gave women the opportunity to reflect on their journey into motherhood, not in isolation, but in relation to the way they themselves were mothered. Like the middle doll in a row of matryoshka dolls (also known as Russian dolls), each mother looked backwards to the women before her, and forwards to the children in front of her.

Mother in the Mother holds the stories of over fifty women who participated in the project, representing a wide diversity of backgrounds and experiences. Read together the stories explore aspects of motherhood and maternal lineage at both a personal 'micro' level and a universal 'macro' level. The basic premise that we asked women: "How does the way in which you were mothered, affect the way you mother your own children?" proved to be endlessly revealing, and of infinite interest. It is a question that is relevant to all mothers, unbounded by class, race, age or situation. And yet we see within the women's writing that it is often the specifics of background and situation that can be so pertinent to the details of the stories.

I have yet to pose this question to any adult (male or female, parent or non-parent) who has not had both an emotional response to the subject and an opinion on the matter. It is a question that I believe will always open up a wide range of responses and experiences. The question, and the project, are at once 'beyond time' and simultaneously specifically grounded in this point in time. I hope that by including my personal story here, and the reasons behind my drive to run the project, I can give you a sense of the micro details behind the bigger project. [2]

Themes

The role of mother is frequently taken for granted. The mother archetype is so fundamental within our lives and to our sense of self, that, as infants and children, we rarely see the person behind the position. Over the project's duration, I had the privilege of hearing stories from a range of mothers. Running through these unique, personal stories are the threads of universal patterns and themes. Some women spoke of how motherhood has transformed their lives and their relationship with their mothers:

We got into a twenty-year battle of miscommunication. But finally we resolved. We found each other. Motherhood brought us together again. It reopened the channels of communication between us.*

Another theme was of women consciously choosing to parent differently:

I want to be different than my mother was. I want my daughter to be able to confide in me and learn positive things from me.*

It became clear through all of the stories that each woman, as she became a mother, found herself either consciously or unconsciously re-evaluating her relationship to her own mother and frequently wanting to reconnect with this relationship in some way.

In her bestselling book *What Mothers Do*, Naomi Stadlen describes how "many women, when they learn they are pregnant, describe an urgent need to contact their own mothers." [3] She explores the roots to this "incredible longing that so many women describe, even those who previously felt estranged from their mothers." [4]

I, myself, had been largely estranged from my mother for some five years prior to the birth of my first daughter. My pregnancy was part of a 'new life', looking into the future and forming a new family with my partner. Yet, from the moment I found out I was pregnant, I craved a mother figure in my life; I found the pain of the lack almost unbearable.

Stadlen breaks this 'longing' down into a range of needs and desires, including the need for mother as 'home': "When a woman bears a baby, she is creating his earliest home, as her mother once created a home for her [...] she may long for the relaxation of being 'at home' with her own mother." [5]

She considers how the daughter, who

may well have been living as an independent woman enjoying a more liberated lifestyle than her own mother, now has a new affinity with her mother, new questions to ask and, in adulthood, new needs as a daughter: "With her own mother, a woman is often returning to a familiar relationship. [...] This is a tested relationship. Now it will have an added dimension. The daughter needs to find out how much she can ask of her mother." [6] [7]

Writing in 1988 Bowlby considered this longing in terms of attachment theory: "No one should be surprised [...] when a woman expecting a baby or a mother caring for young children has a strong desire to be cared for and supported herself. The activation of attachment behaviour in these circumstances is probably universal." [8]

I was gifted with a wonderful mother-in-law and an amazing aunt, but nothing quite filled that direct biological space created by estrangement from my own mother. When a friend and her mother took me shopping for maternity bras, her mum insisted on paying and in that act of generosity I felt the loss acutely. The gravitational pull back to the woman who had carried me through pregnancy was immense.

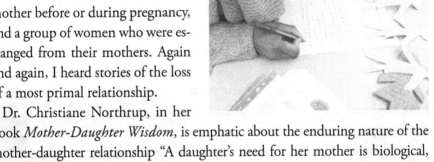

Later, within Mother in the Mother, I worked with a group of women who had lost their own mother before or during pregnancy, and a group of women who were estranged from their mothers. Again and again, I heard stories of the loss of a most primal relationship.

Dr. Christiane Northrup, in her book *Mother-Daughter Wisdom*, is emphatic about the enduring nature of the mother-daughter relationship "A daughter's need for her mother is biological, and it continues throughout her life." [9] She reiterates its primacy, above all other relationships we may have as humans: "Even before birth, our mother provides us with our first experience of nurturing. She is our first and our most powerful female role model. It is from her that we learn what it is to be a woman...Our cells divided and grew to the beat of her heart. Our skin, hair, heart, lungs, and bones were nourished by her blood, blood that was awash with the neurochemicals formed in response to her thoughts, beliefs and emotions." [10]

The women I spoke with confirmed the unavoidable primacy of the maternal relationship. In the words of one:

Your mother represents where you come from. You may not want to replicate this completely with your children, but she is your core, a major part of who you are.*

This concept of mother as 'core', came up repeatedly: mothers (or the lack of) were referred to as "solid ground", "my rock", "compass", "my world". Some women felt that they had been set up for life with the solid foundations of a positive relationship with their mother; others keenly felt the loss of this physical, emotional and spiritual fulcrum.

Whatever our response to this mother-daughter relationship, there is no escaping it. Every new mother was once a woman's new infant. And this is not necessarily a straightforward relationship. As Stadlen observes, "a woman's relationship with her mother has a long history, and is often complex." [11]

Back in 1977 in her book *Of Woman Born*, Adrienne Rich discussed how, "The cathexis between mother and daughter – essential, distorted, misused – is the great unwritten story. Probably there is nothing in human nature more resonant with charges than the flow of energy between two biologically alike bodies, one of which has lain in amniotic bliss inside the other, one of which has labored to give birth to the other. The materials are here for the deepest mutuality and the most painful estrangement." [12]

There is an inherent friction and ambivalence to this relationship, as Nancy Friday explored in the same year in her seminal book *My Mother, My Self.* She charts desires for dependency and independence, for unconditional love and autonomy, attachment and detachment, to please and to reject, to imitate and to individuate.

Friday, Rich, and many others since have explored the rich territory held in the "unique interaction between mother and daughter." [13] It is an ongoing narrative and an interesting dynamic for all women to reflect upon.

Looking backwards, looking forwards

In *Mother in the Mother* I add in a third generation to the traditional mother-daughter relationship dynamic. Told from the point of view of the mother at the centre, each story looks backwards to the woman's past relationship with her mother, and forwards to her relationship with her child. Each writer in the book considers how these different relationships interact and affect each other over time.

Steph Lawler, author of *Mothering the Self*, considers the complexities of being this *centric* woman – simultaneously both mother and daughter: "All mothers are also daughters. Even if the mother is absent, her very absence is likely to assume significance in her daughter's life. And many daughters are also mothers, many of them mothers of daughters. But 'mother' and 'daughter' are radically different positions [...] what if mother and daughter 'inhabit' the same body, what if they are the same person, speaking with two voices?" [14]

The stories within this book allow the centric woman to speak with both of these voices. Rather than rule one another out, the voices layer upon each other, sometimes mirroring, sometimes contradicting, adding subtlety and nuance to this complex role of being at once mother and daughter.

Pregnancy is the only time that we are entirely embodied by, or embody, another human being. The shift from foetus, to infant, to child, to adult, sees the two bodies separating further and further apart. Yet when a woman herself becomes pregnant, it is as if she links directly back into an intact matrilineal network where all the mothers, all the wombs, all the foetuses and infants are connected. This does something peculiar to maternal temporality: it has the ability to stretch time out in linear directions to the distant past and future, and equally to concertina in upon itself to a point that is always in the present. Folding out, folding in, the past and the future, hinged together like delicate butterfly wings. In the way that matryoshka dolls can be opened out and displayed in a long line from smallest to biggest, or packed one inside the other, becoming one body, one space, one time.

Some of the links between the bodies are biological. Mitochondrial DNA (the genetic component of a cell's mitochondria) is passed down on the maternal side, forming a genetic trace between women, far back in history. This gender-specific transfer of DNA, known as 'maternal inheritance', allows people to trace their maternal ancestry. It forms a thread of maternal lin-cage, joining woman, to woman, to woman. [15] "Every daughter contains her mother and all the women who came before her." [16]

It is not only the two bodies that are connected in pregnancy. For within a female foetus, are all the eggs she will ever have. [17] The potential for the next two generations already exists within a woman pregnant with a female foetus. Or, to put it another way, the egg that will become the grandchild, exists within the body of the grandmother if she is pregnant with a girl. This sacred matrilineal trilogy, a body within a body within a body, inspired the title of this book: *Mother in the Mother*. And thus, the concept of looking at all the relationships in this triptych: grandmother, mother and child.

River of maternal love

One of the stories I found most affecting was from a woman who had lost her own mother in childhood:

*I have a strong sense of being deeply loved as a child and I imagine that my 'cup' was overflowing with this love. [...] Consequently, I feel passionately that the more love I can give to my children, the more resources they will have to call upon in the future.**

Although her mother is no longer physically present, the foundation created by their loving relationship continues through her and into her children. I came to think of this as *a river of maternal love*, a flow of compassion moving through one generation into the next.

*I really feel that the love I have for [my son] is the same love my mum poured into me. That the way she loved me directly influences how I love him and how I show my love to him.**

*I realise now that the close loving relationship that I have with my daughter feels very comfortable and familiar because of my mother's and my own relationship, and that is the best thing she has given me**

One woman's mother described the depth of this compassion and connection in the words she gave to her daughter on her wedding day:

When I held your flesh to mine, you melted into my heart and there you *have always stayed. When your heart breaks, so too does mine. When your heart trembles, so too does mine. And when your heart jumps with joy, so too does mine. We are connected.**

I imagine the source of this river of love to run deep through our pasts, rooted in our female ancestors. As with any river it doesn't always flow smoothly: there can be blocks, dams, tributaries, stagnancy, pollution and droughts. Many women wrote about the challenges they experienced growing up:

No one has ever made me feel as worthless as my own mother. She taught me to hate myself.*

My mother is an addict and chronic alcoholic. I spent a lot of my childhood overcome with fear... it swirled inside my stomach constantly and distracted me from my heart and the heart of others. I slowly went numb.*

Again and again the women who were drawn to take part in this project spoke of their determination to change these patterns and reconnect with a river of maternal love.

I was very, very conscious of the wish to not be the cold mother that my mum had been.*

It's clear why my mother is so cold – her mother was exactly the same. It's my biggest fear that I will be that way with my own children, though I try my best to avoid it.*

Mothering differently

Throughout the project I frequently wondered what helped women to make these changes and divert the river back to its source. In doing so, I considered how much these changes are a product of our time. Over the last century we have seen a paradigm shift in the way 'childhood', 'parenting' and 'mothering' are considered: "The start of the twentieth century marked the start in the intensification of mothering, with the family becoming child-centred and departing from childrearing being guided by adult interests [...] childrearing became intensified and motherhood became professionalised. [...] Discourses of good mothering require mothers to spend quality child-focused time." [18]

Since the awareness created by John Bowlby [19] and Mary Ainsworth's [20] work on 'attachment theory' and Winnicott's [21] concept of the 'good enough mother' in the last century, there have been vast changes in styles of parenting advice and practice. Motherhood has become commodified, theorised and institutionalised. Mothers at the start of the twenty-first century are surrounded by a wealth of (often contradictory) professional advice and opinions and values enforced by popular culture – things that our maternal ancestors would not have known. Is it simply that we now better understand the need for significant attachment in healthy child development and are choosing to reverse patterns of 'non-attachment' and authoritarian parenting? [22]

It is impossible to extricate the stories in this book from the period of time, and current understanding of parenting practices in which they were written. However, I think that this desire to divert the river of maternal love back to source  runs much deeper than a current cerebral understanding. One woman's story looked back two generations. She spoke of being the child of a mother who had made just such a transformational change and given her daughter a secure start. This woman in turn was then able to pass this love on to her sons:

> My mother had been neglected terribly as a child…she was physically abused and mentally tortured. My mum grew up feeling completely unloved by her own mother. […] But she always made us feel loved. […] She would wrap her arms around me and I felt safe and loved.*

Terri Apter, psychologist and author of *Difficult Mothers* discusses how "patterns of attachment seem to be passed down from grandmother to mother to child. […] It is difficult to map out new relational pathways. Even when a woman vows to be different from her mother, she may re-enact the familiar and difficult model of mothering she experienced." [23]

Throughout the stories in this book, we see women struggling with just such repeated patterns of behaviour. But, as in the example above, we also hear, again and again, how women succeed in breaking these cycles.

Other mothers

It seems that where needed, women have intuitively and consciously sought ways to try and mother differently. Some of them found *other mothers,* women other than their biological mother to nourish them with their love and care:

*A stronger maternal figure in my life was my grandmother [...] I have many warm memories of her.**

*As a young person I sought guidance and support from older women out-side of my family.**

*My sister was more of a parental figure for me and would check on me and make sure I was eating and looking after myself.**

Stadlen describes how the strength of this need can increase when the woman herself becomes a mother: "Often a motherless new mother will explain how fervently she seeks out experienced maternal women to comfort and reassure her." [24] Throughout my life I have found people who have become maternal figures and from whom I have learnt about loving and mothering. Without the nourishment of these people, I don't think I could have nurtured my own children.

In the ways that the relationship with biological mothers is so primary, some women formed deep attachments to these other mothers:

*I got to spend a lot of time with my child minder 'Aunty Brigid' and her large Irish family. [...] When Brigid died eight years ago, I felt as if I had lost my mother.**

As significant as our biological mother is in her presence or absence, it is fascinating that women can tap in to the flow of maternal love through forming strong attachments to other women. One mother who was adopted as a child describes how, despite finding her biological mother when she was a teenager, *the role of my mum and grandmother was the place of my (adop-tive) mum. [...] I have very fond memories of early childhood. I think I have managed to pass on that nurturing and caring aspect in my own experience of motherhood.**

And one woman, with an adopted child, noticed uncanny non-biological similarities between her child and her mother:

My daughter is very like my mum. They have the same tastes in things already. My daughter is born a week in-between her two grandmothers' birthdays. More and more, my daughter likes to connect with her grandparents without me there.*

I have purposefully avoided the nature/nurture debate in my reflections as I see the two not as distinct but as intricately entwined. [25] However it is clear from these two women's experience that when we refer to our 'mother' and 'grandmother' we may be speaking of the people who form our significant maternal relationships and subsequent nurturing, whether biological or not.

A two-way process of change

However a new child enters a family, there is a profound change that takes place for all involved. It is as if the process of parenting and learning flows in both directions at once: mother and child develop in relationship to one another.

Apter discusses how "as she engages with her infant, a mother's brain too, is stimulated to new growth and learning [...] the complex structures that control our emotions – the limbic system – undergo structural changes as we engage in parenting behavior. [...] As mother and baby interact, each gets smarter." [26]

Another profound point of two-way learning happens at the end of childhood, when we are teenagers and experience a need to separate ourselves from our mother. Sometimes it's a subtle shift, sometimes more dramatic. It's a common theme, almost a rite of passage, maybe a necessary period of individuation.

Many of the women discuss pushing at boundaries as teenagers, separating their beliefs from those of their mothers, pulling back from the relationship to protect themselves, and having a geographical separation. There is a period of adjustment and realignment. Where the mother is able to stand firm in her love during this transition, there is a relationship to return to. The dynamic has changed, but the connection is still there – maybe more boundaried, sometimes even closer than before.

And there is a growing appreciation. Many women see their mother in a new light and frequently value her more than before. From a position of separation, they are able to view their mothers as women in their own right with their own life and struggles, and whose mothering they now recognise and esteem. There is a new understanding and deeper gratitude.

The transition in relationship turns out to be a natural pause for breath and readjustment: one that allows the relationship to develop and flourish.

Unravelling the past

Some women feel the need to make more permanent changes. The concept of breaking a chain, or a cycle, is one of the recurring themes of this book. For some women it is the central tenet of their parenting. Seeing a pattern drawn in their maternal past, something that could repeat ad infinitum if left untouched, they determine to unravel this. They stand at a fulcrum point, looking back to the past, and consciously choosing to do things differently in the future. I wondered: do all women have this choice? Or perhaps change is only possible if we've had the opportunity to pause  and reflect on the past, to bring problematic patterns of behaviour into consciousness? Several women spoke of reaching out for therapeutic help:

*I have always sought the advice and help I need so I can work to break the patterns of the past. [...] I am determined that my daughter will never feel the way I did.**

*When the relationship with my son broke down, I sought professional help – my mum would never have done that.**

Apter considers how "many mothers who themselves experienced deprivation, abandonment, brutality and abuse go on to form a strong and comfortable relationship with their child. Negative cycles can be replaced by a virtuous cycle of positive attachment. The key to breaking the cycle is not to banish the remembering context but to use memory to reflect on and revise responses." [27]

I was consistently awed by the strength of determination these women showed, dealing with desperately painful aspects of their lives to enable the relationship with their children to take a different course. As with many areas of motherhood that can become guilt-ridden, this desire to change the past is no exception, and it seemingly exacerbated some women's sense that they are not 'enough':

I put myself under a ton of pressure, trying to undo my own experience of being a child. [...] I constantly feel I am not giving, being, doing enough. *

But once the will to change is there, these women are incredibly focused:

It fuels my determination to make sure that I break the cycle, or at least alter it slightly, and to ensure that my children are loved and hugged and touched by me on a daily basis. *

In this change lies the potential for deep healing:

[Motherhood] made me tackle issues from childhood as I was fearful not to pass on my issues. It made me really question the parenting I had received, good and bad. Becoming a mother has been a very healing experience. *

Taking part in Mother in the Mother allowed some of these women further opportunity to reflect on their own experiences and revise their responses. Northrup proposes that "if you have a daughter, the work you do to make peace with your own mother and your nurturing history will be the best legacy for health and healing you can pass on to her." [28]

The legacy described here reaches out beyond the next generation, creating positive ripples through all the generations to come.

Grandmothers

It was not only the mothers who made big changes, but in some cases grandmothers as well. To move from mother to grandmother – in effect to move up a generation – is in itself one of life's major transitions. Stadlen describes how "when a baby is born [...] a dense family network of people jostle each other to create enough space for the newcomer." [29]

And Sheila Kitzinger, in her book on becoming a grandmother, discusses how "you are nudged, whether you want it or not, into a different generation. [...] Becoming a grandmother constitutes a life passage." [30] This reshuffle brings a transformative energy, and with it there is rich opportunity for change. It is as if the riverbanks flood for a while, making the ground fertile for the possibility of renewal. Kitzinger wonderfully describes this opening out experience: "The baby represents the continuity of life and the future after you are gone. In a strange way, with the birth of a grandchild, you are yourself reborn." [31]

Many women spoke of how becoming a grandmother seemed to heal something within their mothers:

I love the relationship my daughter has with her grandma. She totally loves her, and fantastically breaks through awkward physical barriers by just clambering on her lap and cuddling her.*

They also noticed that the grandmother/grandchild dynamic was often an easier relationship to navigate and flourish in, than that of mother/child:

I realise what a completely new, happy dimension my children have brought to my mum as well as me. She is really proud of them and I think has a new, better identity as a grandmother.*

Kitzinger describes how becoming a grandmother, like becoming a mother, also opens out the possibility of reflection back to previous generations: "When it is a daughter who gives birth, as you watch her mothering, you remember and relive your own mothering. [...] When you become a grandmother you reflect on the ways in which you were mothered, too." [32]

Matrilineal triptych

What fascinated me throughout the project was not so much the diptych relationships of mother/child or grandmother/child, but the new triptych that was formed between grandmother, mother and child: those three bodies that were once in one body as mother, foetus and egg. An unfolding of linear time and space, from the point of one time, one body, to three bodies: past, present and future.

Our relationship did become closer when I had children. She was more loving as a grandma than she was as a mother and my children loved her.*

Mum is so in love with her. When Mum refers to her as her 'little girl', I want to shout 'but I'm your little girl!' [...] The three of us often spend long days together – Mum is the head matriarch. *

The power of this triptych is palpable: sometimes I notice a woman out with her baby or child, and beside her is her mother. There is something 'complete' in this image that carries a potent energy. Prior to running this project, I would have put this feeling down to my own sense of lack around not having a mother at my side.

But again and again, I heard women talk of the importance, the power, and, at times, the complexity of this three-way relationship:

Since having grandchildren, I have a deeper understanding and compassion for my mum, my daughter and for myself. *

We've learnt side by side how to care for [twins] and [my mother] is already very close to my daughters. *

One thing that almost all the women who took part in this project agreed on, whether they had a loving, challenging or absent relationship with their own mother, was that there is an incredibly strong link between these relationships whether biologically, behaviourally, emotionally or all three:

The way I am as a mother has a direct correlation to the way I was raised by my own mother and the way she was with us was absolutely affected by the way her parents were with her. *

The way I was mothered has definitely affected the way I mother. [...] Since becoming a mother I have felt both a little more compassionate towards my mother, and a little more angry. *

Even the women determined to change patterns of the past, spoke of how strong this behavioural blueprint was, and many women discussed how they would unconsciously repeat patterns and behaviours they had experienced from their mother:

I find myself calling him affectionate names she used to call me without thinking.*

Some traits, unconscious beliefs [...] are funnily similar, probably taking roots in the same genealogical events.*

I often find myself suddenly using phrases that my (adoptive) mum used with me, even after promising I never would.*

It is as if those links that connect us to our mother can never be fully severed: they run far deeper than our conscious selves. At no time does this become more apparent than when we have our own children. We cannot entirely unpick our relationship with our child from our relationship with our mother. One woman summed it up simply by stating:

I am, without doubt, morphing into my mother.*

Healing

There is something in becoming a mother that, in itself, can be healing. I feel that I personally experienced a rich quality of maternal love as a mother, and felt more fully surrounded by 'the maternal', than I did as a child.

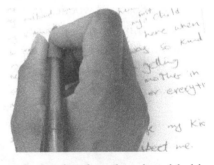

My deep hope and longing at the onset of the project (though I barely dared state this to myself, let alone others) was that through doing this work I would heal my relationship with my own mother. That we would be able to move beyond estrangement and reach that open place back in the hospital waiting room with my daughter loved and held, my nan cared for, all connected; the place of infinite maternal connection that I opened to at the birth of each of my daughters.

But life does not necessarily work like that. The lines of hurt, fear and a need for self-protection run deep on both sides. I personally believe that as Northrup says, "We carry in our own bodies not only our own pain but that of our mothers and grandmothers – however unconsciously." [33]

My physical relationship with my mother is no closer than it was then. Maybe it is even a little more *completely* separated. I recognise that we are each on our own, individual journeys with our own truths and realities. But my relationship with her in my thoughts and in my heart is changing and healing daily, and my relationship with my daughters is so full of love and joy (alongside all the challenges) that I know something, somewhere, is healing.

The beauty of holding space for all these other women, their children, their mothers and their stories of pain, challenge, love and joy has been overwhelming. As the project grew and flourished, it became clear it was not 'my' project, but belonged to all the women involved in it; to all their mothers, grandmothers and their long line of female ancestors; and to all their children and the new lives to come: it was a co-creation. This book is just a pin-point in time, a selection of some of the stories collected between 2012 and 2018. But the resonance of these stories reaches back through the generations far into the past, and forward far into the future.

Working with some of the same women over the course of this project and beyond has given me the privilege of witnessing the changes in these dynamics and relationships. Together, we have created a rich and supportive maternal community, unafraid to reflect on its mothering in light of its maternal lineage. *Mother in the Mother* is in itself a maternal space, holding and honouring these stories, keeping them safe. Stories within stories within stories. They pack up tight together, and unpack and open out, just like a set of brightly painted wooden matryoshka dolls.

I like to think that together we have worked hand in hand to keep the river flowing for the next generation.

Pippa Grace

Notes

[*] All quotations referenced with an asterisk are taken directly from stories within this anthology.

[1] Matryoshka dolls, also known as Russian nesting dolls, or stacking dolls, are a set of wooden dolls of decreasing size that fit one within another. 'Matryoshka' translates as 'little matron'.

[2] Throughout this project I have aimed to consciously use my subjective, personal story as a means to reflect on the wider theme of maternal lineage, in a process of reflexivity described by Charlotte Aull Davies: "Reflexivity, broadly defined, means a turning back on oneself, a process of self-reference [...] Reflexivity at its most immediately obvious level refers to the ways in which the products of research are affected by the personnel and process of doing research." *Reflexive Ethnography – a guide to researching selves and others.* Routledge. Oxon. 2nd edition, 2008. p.4.

I have remained aware that my process is determined in part by my own socio-cultural context, but have aimed to create a diversity of experience through working with a wide range of mothers.

[3] Stadlen, Naomi. *What Mothers Do (Especially When it Looks Like Nothing).* Piatkus. Great Britain. 2004. p.236.

[4] *ibid.* pp.236-237.

[5] *ibid* p.237.

[6] *ibid.* p.238.

[7] See also Stephanie Lawler's discussion of the terms 'mother' and 'child' and how they relate to one another in terms of 'need': "The term 'child' is both an age category and a kinship category. If the (age category 'child' has needs which it is the mother's responsibility to meet, the relationship can be structured by these needs and this responsibility, so that even relationships between mothers and adult children are constituted in terms of what the child needs and what the mother should provide." Lawler, Stephanie. *Mothering the Self – mothers, daughters, subjects.* Routledge. London / New York 2000. p.4.

[8] Bowlby, John. *A Secure Base – clinical applications of attachment theory.* Routledge. London 1988. p.4.

[9] Northrup, Dr. Christiane. *Mother-Daughter Wisdom.* Piatkus. New York. 2005. p.3.

[10] *ibid.* p.6.

[11] Stadlen, Naomi. *What Mothers Do (Especially When it Looks Like Nothing).* Piatkus. Great Britain. 2004. p.235.

[12] Rich, Adrienne. *Of Woman Born – Motherhood as Experience and Institution.* Virago. London 1977. pp.225-226.

[13] Friday, Nancy. *My Mother My Self.* Harper Collins. London. 1994. p.16.

[14] Lawler, Steph. *Mothering the Self – mothers, daughters, subjects.* Routledge. London / New York 2000. pp.3-4.

[15] Northrup, Dr. Christiane. *Mother-Daughter Wisdom.* Piatkus. New York. 2005. pp.61-2.

[16] *ibid.* p.3.

[17] *ibid.* p.5.

[18] Perrier, M. *Middle-Class Mothers' Moralities and Concerted Cultivation: Class Others, Ambivalence and Excess.* 2012. p.656. Perrier discusses the complexities of today's parenting culture and whether class affects how we construct a sense of our own morality as a parent.

[19] John Bowlby was a British psychologist, psychiatrist and psychoanalyst, working from the 1930s until his death in 1990. Bowlby was notable for his interest in child development and for his pioneering work in attachment theory. This theory explores how an infant needs a relationship with at least one primary caregiver for the child's successful social and emotional development, and in particular for learning how to regulate their feelings.

[20] Mary Ainsworth was an American-Canadian developmental psychologist who studied with Bowlby in the 1950s and went on to develop the 'Strange Situation' test in 1965 as a way of assessing individual differences in attachment behaviour by evoking an individual's reaction when encountering stress.

[21] Donald Winnicott, a British psychoanalyst and paediatrician working at a similar time to Bowlby, developed the concept of the "holding environment" where he considered that the foundations of health are laid down by the 'ordinary' mother's loving care of her baby, central to which was the mother's attentive holding of her child. He went on to form the concept of the 'good enough mother' to offset unrealistic idealisation of the 'ordinary mother'.

[22] Bowlby, John. *A Secure Base – clinical applications of attachment theory.* Routledge. London 1988. pp.3-4. Bowlby describes the "set of behavioural patterns which in the ordinary expected environment develop during the early months of life and have the effect of keeping the child in more or less close proximity to its mother" and the consequent "intensity of emotion" that can occur if the attachment is threatened.

[23] Apter, Terri. *Difficult Mothers.* W.W. Norton. New York. 2012. p.175.

[24] Stadlen, Naomi. *What Mothers Do (Especially When it Looks Like Nothing).* Piatkus. Great Britain. 2004. p.243.

[25] See Apter, p.194 on the intimate interaction between nature and nurture.

[26] *ibid* p.26.

[27] *ibid* p.177.

[28] Northrup, Dr. Christiane. *Mother-Daughter Wisdom.* Piatkus. New York. 2005. p.16.

[29] Stadlen, Naomi. *What Mothers Do (Especially When it Looks Like Nothing).* Piatkus. Great Britain. 2004. p.234.

[30] Kitzinger, Sheila. *Becoming a Grandmother, A Life Transition.* Simon & Schuster. London 1997. pp.16-17.

[31] *ibid.* p.17.

[32] *ibid.* p.21.

[33] Northrup, Dr. Christiane. *Women's Bodies, Women's Wisdom.* Piatkus. London. 1995. p.708.

Editors Note

Each story is divided into three sections:

You and Your Child/ren: refers to the mother who is writing the story.

Your Mother and You: refers to the writer's mother, and the writer's experience of growing up.

Your Mother, You, Your Child/ren: refers to the relationships between the mother who is writing, her mother, and the writer's child/children.

All stories are shared anonymously and written in the women's own voices.

All photographs are of Mother in the Mother participants and their families, with permission. The image used next to any piece of writing does not imply authorship of the writing.

Deeply
Connected

Motherhood is frequently sold to us as an exemplum of a pure, peaceful, unconditional love. The stories here describe the incredibly deep bonds that can exist between mothers and their children as made of much tougher stuff.

There can be a fierceness to a mother's love, an animal-like strength and protectiveness. One woman describes being like a 'lioness' fending off 'jackals' when she finds out she is pregnant. And there can be layers of complexity: the love may be unconditional, but it is not necessarily peaceful or painless. The relationship may contain its fair share of struggles and challenges.

Like a great tree, with a network of immensely deep roots, the connection between mother and child demonstrated by these stories is able to withstand this above-ground turbulence. Its branches move in life's day-to-day weather and occasional storms, but it remains firmly rooted. Women who experience this connection with their mother appear to be held in a safety net woven of many-stranded love. They speak of being connected by 'apron strings', 'positive energy', 'the same beliefs and values' and 'sleeping in the same bed when we were young'. These connections not only nourished them as children, but continue to do so throughout their adult lives – never more so than when they themselves become mothers.

In these stories we see love spill out from one generation into the next: a new grandmother holds a deep love for her daughter, and now they share the experience of motherhood and the love for the new child. This child has not only their mother to lean back into, but also their grandmother. The child is deeply rooted. New mothers talk about wanting to emulate the positives they have learnt from their own mothers.

All exist in relationship to one another.

All are deeply connected.

My New Normal

"Your job is to show her the world, not to be her world." This is what my partner said to me in the first week of our daughter's life, when he saw me more scared than he'd ever seen me before. I got so frustrated by the constant questions of, "Do you love her?", "Are you enjoying it?" How was I meant to answer these questions? I'd only just met her! Now I know it's okay to have mixed emotions about motherhood.

From the moment she was born I was constantly trying to get back to 'normal'. It took me several months to realise that she was the 'new normal', and that was actually quite good. She teaches me to look at the world in a different way, to slow down and see the world with new, sparkly eyes. I've never seen anyone so happy to start the day: she bounds with joy and enthusiasm. She is happy to be alive and just happy to be with me. Sometimes her wriggliness annoys me. I just want to say, "Be calm and just hug me." But she's got other things on her mind!

Who can blame her? After all, she really does take after me! I had a really healthy and active pregnancy and consequently I rarely sat down: jogging here, cycling there, places to go for me… and now for her too.

Mum was young when she had me and quite idealistic. Her idealism is a trait that she has taught me. It hasn't always served me well, but I wouldn't be me without it, and Mum wouldn't be her without it.

When I was about ten my mum worked in a children's centre. A child she had to look after there had AIDS. This was the 1980s, and AIDS was still a bit unknown. Mum's other colleagues were nervous to look after the child. I remember being so proud of my mum, she didn't hesitate in nurturing the child. When I was fourteen, I wrote a story about this for school. When I was sixteen, I ripped the story up in a rage, when I was furious at Mum after we'd clashed. When I was eighteen, I taped the story back together when I felt love towards her again! I think this event goes some way to symbolising my feelings about my mum: pride and fury.

After not living near Mum for a decade, she moved down the road from me a few years ago. I was thrilled that I finally had the chance to be physically and emotionally close to her. This really manifested itself when I was pregnant. I can often be too quick to discard Mum's wisdom and advice, but this time I was determined that I would really try to listen and learn from her.

This began from the moment I gave birth to the next generation of women in our family. My mum was the first person to dress my daughter. She even looked like Mum! She calls Mum the same nickname I called Mum's mum, and so the cycle continues. Mum is so in love with her. When she refers to my daughter as 'her little girl', I want to shout, "But I'm your little girl!" I often think that Mum's favourite part of seeing me is seeing her. The three of us often spend long days together.

Mum is the head matriarch. I have a lot of respect for my mum and the way she raised me, she is relaxed and trusting…but I sometimes wish I had a mum that backed down when she was wrong: I think this would have served me well in life. I hope I can give this to my daughter. I was always quite anxious about having a little girl, as Mum is strong-willed and determined…and so am I! The upside of this was that Mum always let me be me, but this also made us clash badly over the years. I'm pretty sure that I too am raising a girl of a similar nature. Already there are signs. Should I counter balance it? Do I want to change it? Should I just let it be?

The Best Job in the World

I really wanted to be a mother, and my first child was very planned and very wanted. I had a straightforward pregnancy and a lovely birth. My son came three weeks early. We were doing a house renovation, and the day I went into labour we had just had our hot water connected. We had no hospital bag, no baby car seat, only one baby outfit…we were a bit unprepared and that's how it stayed for the first six months!

I struggled with sleep deprivation and breastfeeding a long-term jaundiced baby. In desperation, I turned to a book someone had recommended to me in pregnancy. In hindsight, I wish I had never read this book, it made me feel like a failure as a mum: I just didn't fit her mould. It took me a long time, probably until the birth of my second child, to recover from the feelings of failure. Luckily, I met one amazing friend who helped me find my way to being the mummy I wanted to be.

I love being a mother: I have the best job in the world. It's tough and tiring, but what other job rewards you with the biggest cuddles, the funniest sayings and pure, unconditional love every day?

My mother is a big, soft cushion covering a solid, sturdy rock. She was always there for me as a child and as an adult, but at the same time she has a slight fragility that makes me want to protect her.

When I was young, my mum was the main breadwinner as my dad went back to university. I remember her as someone always doing something, she always found time to cook from scratch, grow food and make clothes.

I only remember a few times of conflict, mainly where I was winding my mum up. With a nearly six-year-old tweeny I'm on the receiving end now and I can appreciate her despairing at me! I also used to wish my parents weren't so strict, especially wanting to stop me growing up so fast. I'm finding myself wanting to parent in a lot of the same ways that my mum did.

As long as I can remember I've always been terrified at the thought of losing my mum. Because of this I've never wanted to stray too far and cut those apron strings. I really appreciate them and I love now being best friends with my mum. I like to speak to her every day on the phone, even if I know I'm going to see her on the same day (it drives my husband nuts).

I love the fact she has taken on a really active role as granny, it's brilliant seeing my boys be really close to her too. Special time for me is pottering down the allotment with her and my boys, chatting about things as we dig the soil and plant veg. I hope when my children are older they will like me as much as I like my mum.

This, Too, Is Love

When I was fifteen, I wrote an English essay entitled 'A Woman's Place is in the Home?' All I remember of the piece is being indignant that women were expected to stay at home with the children when there were alternatives available. I think, in part, I was influenced by my own upbringing, having been raised by a young, single mother who worked nights as a nurse to support her two children.

I couldn't know then that returning to work, when my daughter was just six months old, would weigh heavy on my heart. That nursing sick patients, when my own child was unwell and needed tending, was unthinkable. That I would instinctively want to hold her close, sleep with her nestled in the crook of my arm, feed her from my body. I couldn't know then that having three home-birthed, water babies would wake me up to the power of surrender, of trusting and flowing with life. Home is the place where I gladly spend most of my days, knowing, deep in my bones, that raising my children is the best job I've ever had and the only one I ever really knew that I wanted.

Two words come to mind when I see my mother through child's eyes: hair and food. I remember her wide-toothed, long-handled, afro comb and the perfectly rounded halo that took time to get just so. I would sit cross-legged on the floor whilst she greased up my hair, struggling to tease a comb through the kinky frizz. Tears pricked my eyes when plaiting fingers snagged a strand and pulled my scalp: I'm not sure it was always accidental.

As for food, there was daily cooking from scratch. Lots of spice, some unusual ingredients, the terrifying whistle and snort of the pressure cooker steaming the overnight-soaked black-eyed peas into submission. Summers were beach trips with picnics of home-made coleslaw and chicken drumsticks cooked up at the crack of dawn. Christmas brought with it turkey stew with dumplings and a delicious, beautifully iced, igloo cake complete with skating penguins and tiny snow peaks. Pure magic.

Visits with my mother haven't always been easy. Though I'd encouraged her to accept a job near the Caribbean island she still called home, I felt a little unmoored when she left just a few short weeks after I met my now-husband. Once we'd wed, I felt my mother's absence keenly. There were a smattering of visits when my children were small. These occasions spawned feelings of criticism: resentments, tears, harsh words. We disappointed each other and felt let down.

So, when she wanted to stay at mine, offering to help when my husband was away for a week last year, it was with slight trepidation that I accepted. However, from the moment she swept in, she was just the pause we needed. There was an ease and a fluidity between us that had been missing for a while. We were in sync. And when I caught sight of my mother brushing my daughter's hair, I realised that this, too, is love.

I Followed Her Everywhere

I met my husband in Egypt. When I got back to Sudan, I found out I was pregnant. It was easy because I was with my sisters and brothers. But by my second pregnancy we were back in England. This was a much more difficult pregnancy, I was very sick.

After my second birth I stayed with my sister in London for a month. My third birth was a caesarean and my sister visited me, but could only stay for a week.

I have a very strong relationship with my mother. I am the seventh of her nine children. And she is the first daughter of eleven brothers and eleven sisters.

When I had my children, I realised how hard my mum had worked in labour. Soon after the birth, my dad called me and asked how I felt. I told him that I now realised how tired my mum had been: I understood.

My mother is a very strong woman and a hard-worker, she is also very kind and caring. When she first got married and came to her house there were eighteen people already living there. She had to look after them before she could have her own children.

As we grew up, I was the closest one to my mum: we went out a lot and I followed her everywhere. She was very affectionate, we slept in the same bed with her when we were young and if we were ill. Our relationship stayed strong as I grew older.

I have three daughters. They call my mother, Mum! They are really close and video call Sudan every two or three days. My oldest daughter says that she remembers my mum's face from when she was in Sudan. My younger children have never met her, but even so they are very close.

My mum isn't educated, and I have a degree, but we parent very similarly. The way she was definitely affected the way I mother. I try to follow how she mothered. If I get angry with my girls, I try to stop and remember how my mum and dad were with us. They never beat us.

I teach my children the same way my parents taught us. I find the hardest thing about being a mum is making my children follow the same path in life that we do.

She Loves Her So Beautifully

I grew up in a family of four children and loved being part of a reasonably big family. From a young age I knew that I wanted to work with children and pursued a career as an Early Years teacher.

My husband and I decided to start trying for a family. Although I knew that it can take a long time for some couples to conceive, there was a part of me that thought I might follow in my mother's footsteps and conceive fairly quickly. I knew that I was pregnant two weeks after we decided that we would start trying to conceive and felt completely calm and utterly thrilled about it.

Labour was the most exhausting and empowering thing I have ever done. I planned to have a home birth, and although I had to be transferred to hospital after labouring for eighteen hours, I was incredibly thankful for the care I received from some wonderful midwives. I am so aware of how fragile pregnancy and labour can be, and the experience of giving birth to my daughter has humbled me greatly.

I absolutely loved those early weeks of carrying my newborn baby around in a sling, snuggled in close to me. She was incredibly content and calm, and I honestly didn't want the newborn phase to end.

Motherhood often challenges my patience and makes me constantly re-evaluate my priorities and the decisions that I make. The paradoxes of parenthood never cease to perplex and amaze me.

I have a deep respect for my mother and her devotion to raising me and my siblings with a grace and kindness that has taught me a lot over the years. She made the decision not to work while raising us, and my presiding memory is of an incredibly calm and patient woman, always willing to share her knowledge and understanding with us. Her parenting was always very considered and gentle, but with clear and consistent boundaries.

As a teenager, my home felt like a safe haven for my friends to come to, and there was always room for one more around our dining table. As an adult I now appreciate that I created a lot of extra work for my mum, but she never once made me feel like I couldn't invite friends to eat with us at short notice. In my teens, I made life fairly difficult for my parents, and although I knew that some of my life choices were upsetting for them, I never felt pushed away or disconnected from them.

When I moved away from home to university, my relationship with my mother strengthened a lot, and she continues to be a great encouragement and inspiration to me.

Since having my daughter, a year ago, I have thought a lot about how I was mothered, and I have an even deeper respect and love for my mother and father in the way they gave me so much of their time, selflessness, patience and love. I have also reflected a lot on the dynamics within my family that I find challenging, and how I would like to do things differently with my husband in the way that we raise our daughter.

I remember when my mum came to visit us when my daughter was six weeks old. My daughter was lying on a quilt and as my mum bent down to her level and smiled at her, my baby smiled at her for the first time, which brought tears to my mother's eyes. It was beautiful to witness her love and enjoyment of my daughter in that moment.

I have loved seeing my mum embrace her role as a grandmother, and she is so encouraging of the way that I mother my daughter, which I am very grateful for. I have such fond memories of my maternal grandmother, and I am truly thankful that my daughter has a wonderful grandmother who loves her so beautifully.

We Share the Experience of Mothering Now

My transition into motherhood has felt slow. I feel like I am only just seeing myself and understanding myself as a mother, three years and two children on. I see my girls laughing in hysterics at their own private jokes and I see that I am their mum, they are separate from me and interact with the world in their own ways.

The first birth was excruciatingly late and long, but I had her at home without any intervention and felt empowered by my strength and willpower. I came out of it on a high. The second birth was, in contrast, shockingly short (but no less powerful) and again at home. My two daughters were born in exactly the same place in our kitchen, I was so quietly proud of myself. My husband was in awe and we were, all of a sudden, four.

The greatest challenges for me have slowly crept in, as my daughters get older and have stronger opinions and try to assert themselves. I realise how little time I have to myself and I have found an anger I didn't know was there. It runs out of me and shouts at my daughter. It wants her to go away and give me quiet. It wants her to do what I want her to do, to just let me be in control. It is fierce and scares me. I am trying to find a balance in me, a way of letting go a little more, but still holding my girls close.

My mum was in control, she was the boss, but she was also quite liberal and gave me lots of space to make mistakes and do my own thing. My sister said recently that she was always there for us if we needed her but never too close: she didn't hug and snuggle, but she also didn't smother.

In her kitchen there was mess and order all at once, and as we fostered there were always children everywhere. The back door was always open.

I remember the exact moment I broke away from my mum and realised she was not always in charge. We were brought up as Catholics and would go to church every Sunday. One morning when I was fourteen, I asked to stop the car on the way home from church and said that I didn't want to go again. I was terrified to tell her, of disappointing her or abandoning something she felt was important. She took it well, in her logical and liberal way: it was my decision to make.

My mum had a serious neck and back problem as I was growing up and I will always blame it for her lack of physical closeness. Hugs felt, and still do feel, awkward. I love cuddling my children, I hope they carry on letting me.

My mum was at the birth of my first daughter. She waited with me for three weeks and jumped up and down with me in Leigh Woods to try and get my waters to break (which worked!). She recognized transition and let me swear in her face. She held my hand while I pushed. She comforted my husband. She saw my baby's head first. It was amazing to have her there.

She gave me a card when she left to go home, and it made me realise that our relationship had shifted. We share the experience of mothering now. I see vulnerability in her that I never saw before. The mistakes she feels she made in the way she raised us, the tentative way she offers advice or opinions. She doesn't have it all sewn up, she isn't in control.

I see her becoming older and slower and I feel that shift that people talk about, when the parenting tables turn and you start to care for your parents. My mum is a brilliant grandmother. I think my children see her quite classically as fun and scary at the same time.

Always in Their Hearts

I was thirty when I had my first child. Growing up with older siblings and having helped them look after their babies made me think I was going to be a super mum some day. When my baby arrived, I gave up my life of nightclubbing and going out and started a new life with my family.

I had all this love and strength and I kind of knew what to expect. But it took me a while to realise that I'm the baby's mother all the time, and that the baby is here all the time. I was trying to do my best and felt tired and overprotective; I could not let someone else be with my baby.

I grew up with my mum, dad and six other siblings. My mum only had my father to help her out after he came home from work. She was loving and taught us how to look after ourselves. She always made sure we were safe. I remember my mother's mother was very old but very active. She would always tell us stories and helped us learn how to do chores.

My mother lives in Namibia so we don't see her very often, but my children speak on the phone with her. The last time I went home was with my oldest son, when he was one. It was so nice to see them together. Even though he was quite big and my mother is quite old, she wanted to carry him everywhere, it was like making up for lost time. We were there for a month and my child could tell this was 'home'. My other children are all keen to see her, they call her KuKu which means 'grandma'. She is always in their hearts.

Unchosen
Decisions

Life rarely runs in straight lines. We may be sent challenges that shake our foundations and disrupt the narrative we think we have written for our lives. So many parts of parenting, pregnancy and birth are unchosen, we do our best with the cards we are dealt. There is a mythical idea of 'choice' surrounding birth – choosing to conceive, choosing how to birth, choosing how many children…whereas many women's experiences are not based on choice but dealing with what happens. So much of life, especially bringing it into the world and nurturing it, is far beyond our control. What if we get pregnant before we are ready, when we are not living where we expected to be, or when we already have a full family? What if we thought we could never conceive only to then get pregnant, or see two heartbeats rather than one on a routine scan? Sometimes the life we thought we were leading turns on its axis and takes us on a completely unexpected path.

These are times when everything is shaken up, nothing seems stable, and we may have to make decisions we never previously considered. When a woman has a deep-rooted attachment to her own mother, her ability to withstand and deal with this shifting ground may be stronger. If her primal relationship is secure, dealing with such changes, especially when they involve her bringing new life into the world, may seem daunting but do-able. Without this foundation, the threat to her sense of self and her life may be overwhelmed by these changes. All of these women talk of digging deep into their emotional and physical reserves to find what they needed to help them through these shifting times.

Getting Through the Maze

When we conceived our daughter, it was pretty miraculous. We were using contraception which failed, and so I took the morning-after pill. I gave it no more thought… until I didn't have a period. I was absolutely astonished when a pregnancy test was positive.

My boyfriend and I were both in our mid-twenties, still living in a shared house and had only been together for a year. We were committed and happy, but we weren't ready for this. He was unsure. And I was too… for about twenty-four hours. Then I had absolute unwavering clarity: I was going to have this baby no matter what. I was like a lioness, and any attempts he made to discuss the 'possibilities' were fended off like jackals. I feel for him now, having his future decided like that, but at the time I could do nothing but defend the rights of my already precious, tenacious, little child.

We had hypnobirthing classes together and it gave us a chance to process the change and focus our lives on our journey into parenthood. We bought a home and moved in two weeks before she was born, in our bedroom. It made us united and confident as parents.

We have lapsed into very traditional roles, in spite of being quite liberal people. That has affected my sense of identity possibly more than being a mother. The relentless domestic chores can wear me down and I have found it hard to carve out time for myself. But my relationship with my children and my ability to engage with them has increased my confidence and self-worth.

My mother is very much in my life. She was young when she became a parent: nineteen when she had my brother and twenty-five when she had me. She struggled when I was little. She felt lonely and frustrated and left my dad when I was five. We always had contact, but there was a sense that she wasn't really available for a while.

As my children reach that age, I consider what it must have felt like to move out and leave us. I find it hard to imagine being able to do that myself. I think I grew up a bit too fast. I became very self-reliant, responsible and dependable. I was naturally supportive and caring towards my mum. She was a very liberal parent and used trust, honesty and accountability as her disciplinary tools. My mother is a good woman.

I definitely appreciate my mother more now that I am a parent myself. She was clearly very loving, tender and affectionate to me; it is something I know in my body and can share with my own children. "I love you" flows very easily for me.

When my parents re-married they both brought step-siblings into the family. It meant that there was very little simple family time, it all had to be negotiated. Being with mum now with my two daughters gives us back that family time. She is respectful and honest with me and supports me as a parent. I think I am more mature as a parent than she was. My relationship with my children gives them a lot more space to be children. I am more conscious and less reactive than she could be when I was little, I often felt she needed my support as much as I needed hers. She is now quite straight-forward to be with. She is creative and fun with my children.

In some respects, I think I am very like my mum, in how I find my way intuitively rather than following too many rule books. Perhaps I just have more inner resources for getting through the maze.

An Unexpected but Happy Surprise

I was twenty-five when I became pregnant with my first daughter and it was an unexpected but happy surprise. I lost contact with lots of friends, as I was the only one having a baby and my lifestyle changed almost instantly.

I loved being a mother and loved being a family, but felt a loss of some parts of my life: the friends I didn't see much of and the career I thought I wanted and then had to step away from.

I became quite anxious about lots of things and had panic attacks in the first year of being a mother. It wasn't diagnosed, but my partner thinks I had postnatal depression for a while. I think this was about adjusting to my new life. I had no idea about how intense having a baby could be and how lack of sleep changes everything!

As for rewards, it's just the best thing ever to have children, they are so funny and loving and they really motivate me to do the best I can, as I want to give them the best of me. They trust me to do this and hopefully it will be good enough. It has also really helped me form a deeper relationship with my partner, having children has made us work on this.

My memory of my mum was that she was nearly always distracted by a tricky relationship with my dad. She did show me love, and I remember this mostly when I was poorly; she was good at looking after me when I was ill. Other than that, she was busy with day-to-day chores and they seemed to carry a certain anxiety for her. When I was eight, my mum's mum died and she was devastated. Sadness prevailed and I never felt so connected to her after that.

I always felt that I wanted to protect my mum and I began to feel as though I had to look after her before I became a teenager. She was very accepting of people, or seemed to be. She is a bit more assertive now, which is great, and I get on well with her, although there is still a sense that I need to protect her.

I became closer to my mum when I had children. When I had my first child, we spent quite a lot of time together, it was much happier and healing all round I think.

From the moment my daughter was born, I became a worrier. I hadn't been one before, but I suddenly changed my feelings about what I was prepared to do, and allow people to do with my baby.

Now my children are older I am letting go more as I see them becoming independent and capable. I think I have allowed my children to express their emotions more than I felt I could when I was younger.

My mum has a good relationship with my children. She likes to spoil them and loves their company. Writing this I realise what a completely new, happy dimension my children have brought to my mum, as well as to me. She is really proud of them and I think has a new, better identity as a grandmother.

I Wanted to Be an Earth Mother

Cursed with polycystic ovaries, I was told, "You will find it extremely difficult to get pregnant." This was not the case. In the space of six months I had met my husband and my stepdaughter-to-be, and become pregnant!

Although I was over-joyed to be growing a new life, fear sat next to me regularly. My stepdaughter was with us every weekend, and for my husband I was carrying his second child. Heavy in the air around my in-laws was the knowledge that I represented the distraction from 'the break-up', and so I retreated into myself, to protect the connection with the miracle that was transforming me.

We lived in the top of a farmhouse. That sounds idyllic, but in reality it swarmed with mice, rats, flies and at one point a bloated dead cow, out in the farmyard. The house itself had a long path that the cows walked along to get milked, the path was often packed with their manure, and it felt as if I lived in a twisted fairy tale, hidden in the turrets of a darkened house. It wasn't long before we moved away and life grew more colourful, but the shadow effect of those early days stuck to my skin for months.

Me and my mum lived alone for a short while, after my dad left when I was three. I remember that time as glorious. She was young and rebellious: we would paint with our fingers, open Christmas presents before Christmas, and laughed a lot. Our time together felt free and decadent. I knew she loved me.

I was aware my mum made sacrifices for me. We were poor and she would go without food so I could eat my fill. She would wear her shoes until they had holes, so I could have new school shoes.

I hadn't realised she needed anyone else, until she met my dad, the man who brought me up. My mum became a new creature, with perfume and red dresses, talking of nights out and 'good behaviour'. Our lives shifted in size: we changed from being free-range vegetarians to a Sunday roast eating family. As time passed, she became surrounded by toddlers and I preferred the company of strangers. She became a keeper of my secrets and I was her link to rebellion. At times our connection has grown faint and has felt imaginary. Mostly, though, she is a purple-wearing, play-loving woman, and I love her.

Play and freedom of expression have always been a priority with my children and family. I believe those values were nurtured by my mum when I was little. As a consequence, my home is stuffed full of creative projects, artwork, poetry and writing. I wonder if my children will be drawn to a less chaotic environment as they grow up, as an act of rebellion. Time will tell.

When I became a mother, my mum and I were not so close. I had lived abroad for a while and she had a busy family of her own. There followed a time when our roles had to be re-defined and I found that hard. It took me some time before I learnt to mother myself and my children enough to separate my needs from our relationship.

As my children have grown, relationships and expectations have become easier to manage. I am grateful for the happy silliness we share together as a family: a love of animals, peace, respect for the planet, unexpected beauty, rude jokes and raucous laughter are all things my children, my mum and I share. I reckon we are all pretty lucky.

Two Heads Are Better Than One

As soon as my husband and I heard the sonographer say, "I can see two heart-beats," our world changed forever. Shock, disbelief and joy hit us in waves. We quickly began a journey of monitoring our baby girls' growth every fort-night under the care of our consultant. At every turn we were warned of risks: twin-to-twin transfusion syndrome, growth restriction, amniotic fluid issues, anaemia, the list goes on. But despite all the concerns, our girls shared their placenta beautifully and each baby grew at a lovely pace.

But at week thirty-two, during a routine scan, I became ill and was admit-ted to the antenatal ward. Six days in hospital later, I was told that the girls would need to be delivered by C-section that day. There was no choice but to go ahead and hope for the best.

At 19:26 and 19:27 our girls were delivered. As each baby took their first breath and let out a cry, I felt instant relief wash over me: everything was going to be okay.

Our girls spent thirty days in NICU. They were tremendously resilient to all the changes bestowed upon on them, from starting life in an incubator, to being fed through a tube and handled by multiple nurses. My husband and I cared for them in amongst the wires and machines every day until we could finally bring them home. It was quite possibly the most exciting and terrifying day of both our lives. It is wonderful to finally feel like a family, as we look towards the future together, stronger than ever.

My mother is an amazing woman. She has always been there for me for a hug, advice, or simply to listen. She has been an exceptional role model in kindness, love and patience throughout my life. As a child, I recall a sense of security and happiness as we cuddled up on the sofa, or played on the beach together.

Since becoming a mother, our relationship has taken on a whole new dimension. We have had lengthy discussions where I have broken down under the weight of new motherhood and she has hugged me and reassured me. I feel forever indebted to her for her kindness and honesty. I have been shocked by how the reality of motherhood is played down, but my mum has been there to discuss with me the warts and all, as I try to make sense of it.

As a mother to twins, you need as much help as you can get, and my mother has been there to support us, from cooking home-made meals to fuel us during our long days and nights in NICU, to changing countless nappies and even staying over so my husband could sleep. We've learnt, side by side, how to care for two.

Although I realise I cannot possibly emulate her, I would like to feel I can take some of the good behaviours she showed towards me: compassion, love, understanding, and apply this to the way I raise my own children. I want them to feel the love and security that I did, and have the freedom to enjoy their childhood together.

Ideal and Reality

I had a clear idea of how I wanted to raise my children: I would be living close to nature in a small, mutually supportive community – 'Little House on the Prairie' style. This was slightly in conflict with my reality at the time, living in a flat in London around the corner from the 'Murder Mile'.

My mother, sisters and old friends were overseas, so I didn't have immediate physical support except from my partner who was very supportive but exhausted. So, I was on the phone a lot, engaging them and the breastfeeding hotline in lively debates about which breast to feed from next. I also kept a poo diary with timings and colour and texture descriptions. I had changed overnight from an easy-going and laid-back young woman, to an irritable, anxious, perfectionist.

The central issue for me in raising children has been the conflict between the ideal and the reality of our existence. But with experience – and the birth of my second child – I have mellowed and realise that acceptance of reality is much better than trying to construct a fantasy.

My mother and I have always been close. She was warm and loving, and mostly enjoyed being a mum. I was the youngest of three girls and her 'baby'. She didn't have a good relationship with her own mother who was very critical.

My mother has always been anxious. When I was ten, she had a breakdown and was hospitalised with anxiety and depression. I learned to adapt to whatever mother she presented to me. Sometimes she was her 'normal' self and we would pick up where we left off, sometimes she was her 'anxious' self and I would hold back so as not to worry her and to protect my feelings as well. It sounds a bit strange written down, but it is a seamless transition and I can tell how she is over the phone immediately.

When I was around seventeen, I told her that I would have to pull back from her to protect myself. This boundary has helped us to stay close and loving.

My mother is very loving and caring with my children and genuinely enjoys being their grandmother. As a grandmother, she says that she doesn't have the worries that she had as a mother. She has read loads of books to them and most of our children's books are from her. She has always confidently looked after my children and reassured my new mother anxieties.

I realise now that the close, loving relationship that I have with my daughter feels very comfortable and familiar because of my mother's and my own relationship, and that is the best thing she has given me.

Overwhelmed by Love and Tiredness

I was young when I became a mother. I think that made things easier for me as I didn't have many expectations or preconceptions.

My first pregnancy was very straightforward and wonderful. The first few weeks with my son were luscious. I was overwhelmed by love and tiredness. Being a mother felt like the most incredible honour. I had gone through the initiation into motherhood and it was beautiful.

I went on to birth a daughter two years later. We were so pleased to have a boy and girl and we thought our family was complete. But two years after that another daughter graced us with her arrival.

The greatest rewards are the heart opening experiences of motherhood, the meaning and purpose it brings. The greatest challenge of early motherhood was without doubt tiredness. I look back now and realise how completely worn out I was, having three pre-school aged children before I was thirty. When our third baby was born, we were running a family business and that was tough. This challenge led to a really difficult decision. The next pregnancy was too much, and we decided to terminate, as I really felt it would have pushed me too far.

When I was a child, I took my mother for granted. My mum was a very busy woman. She worked full time and looked after my brother, me and my disabled father. She always seemed to have more important things to do and often wanted to be by herself. She was an only child and I think she needed that alone time, but I didn't understand that when I was a child. She used to shut herself in the kitchen listening to Radio 4 and try to work. She didn't like cooking, probably because she came home from a full day of work, then felt the burden of having to feed the family.

My grandmother on the other hand was an amazing cook. Plying us with food was the way she showed her love. My grandmother was a huge cuddly woman with big, voluptuous breasts and a big smile. Her work was her family and home.

My mum was beautiful and slim and often appeared stressed. I wish I had helped her more. I didn't realise how tired she must have been. When she was in her forties, she became quite ill with fibroids and had a hysterectomy. I ignored how hard it must have been for her, I was too young to understand the significance of this operation for her as a woman.

My mum had an amazing curiosity about life and science, and she sparked my interest in the world. She always encouraged us and used to tell us that we could achieve anything in life. She taught us so many life-skills and always seemed to have an answer to our questions and worries.

Sometimes I just wanted her to tell me she loved me, I don't think she ever said it.

I felt very secure at home, but I often wanted to push the boundaries. I rebelled as a teenager and wanted total freedom and didn't want my mum to know what I was doing. I knew she wouldn't approve, so I became very secretive and shut her out. She waited patiently for me to grow up: it felt like it took years for her to forgive me.

When I had children, I understood what hard work it is to be a mother, but also how rewarding it is: it's worth the effort! I also understand that there is no right way to be a mum, there is just reacting in the moment, spontaneously. Sometimes I mess up, feel guilty for something I've said or done, but I always try to learn from it and not make the same mistake again. My mum never criticises the way I do things and never interferes, she never tells me what to do or how to do it. She celebrates our successes and is happy for my achievements.

Sometimes, my friends and I catch ourselves saying, "Gosh, I'm turning into my mother!" as if that is a bad thing. But, really, I would love to have my mum's strength, wisdom and resilience. I hope I am becoming more like her. My children love her to bits, and so do I.

Young

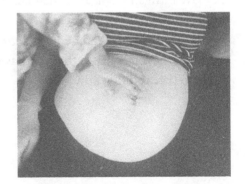

What is it like to be a young mother in an environment where people are increasingly having children later in life? [†] During this project, young mums were defined as women who'd had their first birth aged twenty or under. In their writings, some of these women talk about how they have, at times, felt judged and stigmatised by others. Some discuss feeling out of step with their contemporaries. However, their emphasis is frequently on the positive aspects of their lives. They talk about the immense joy their children bring them and the importance they place on family values.

One result of being a young mum is that their own mothers may well become young grandmothers. All of the generations are closer together in age and, at times, more closely bonded. Grandmothers may become closely connected to their grandchildren and more involved in their day-to-day care than where there is a wider age gap. Young mums are still close in age to their own position as child and daughter, and talk of the support from their mothers as they give birth and look after their children. These young women reflect back on their own upbringings with a maturity that may have manifested when they became mothers. Some have a growing appreciation of their mothers, whilst one now recognises that she was wrongly treated as a child and determines to parent differently.

....

[†] In 2017 the average age for first time mothers in England and Wales was 28.8. In 1975 it was 24.2 (Office for National Statistics)

I Never Knew

I was never quite prepared to be a mum. It was towards the end of my first year of university at Bournemouth when I found out that I was pregnant. I had this strange craving for seafood and went out and got crab. That night I had an awful bellyache. I was tossing and turning all night and it felt like there was an alien in my tummy trying to get out: I honestly thought I had been possessed and was going to die. Now I realise it was my daughter saying, "Hey, I'm here! Don't eat that stuff, it's bad for me!" The next day I woke up, relieved not to be dead or have an alien popping out of me. However, there was a distinctive bump and my PJs were ripped. I went to my friend, stood side on and was like, "Does it look like I'm pregnant?"

I went straight to get a test and doctors confirmed I was sixteen weeks in. I asked Uni for a delay for my final exams, to take the summer while I figured things out. A couple of months later my partner and I were back in Bournemouth, me for end of year exams, him for job interviews. We scanned the newspapers for the cheapest flat. It was all a whirlwind. But when my daughter was born, I loved her so much and she made me become the woman I am now.

My mum was always the strict one growing up. We didn't really get on at all for a while when I was a teenager. I know she didn't always agree with my choice of friends. I remember her always asking me to come home after being on a night out with friends. I used to think at the time, "Why is she punishing me? Why doesn't she want me to have any fun?" Now I think she probably just wanted to spend time with me.

As a child, though, I always remember she was the one on my side. She was the one making sure I had everything I needed for school. She was always the sensible, orderly one, and always the one you could rely on to get things sorted out. I think that this is true in many families. Even though many women now go to work, they still, in most cases I've witnessed, take on the majority of the traditional maternal roles as well, doing two jobs.

I never knew how much my mum loved me. It seems obvious for a child to know that, but even after having and loving my own daughter so much, I just didn't realise until the day my mum gave me this letter on my wedding day. [You can read it on the following page.]

I never really understood what it was like for her having me so young. I was told stories, but this letter was a true insight: her story to me through her eyes. The line about her living as I have lived made me see all that I mean to her, now and throughout my life. To me it changed how I saw my mum: I see her as part of me. People used to always say how my mum was full of life, loud and spirited just like me when she was a teenager. My mum used to say it changed when she had me because she had to grow up quickly and be responsible. I now believe all her positive energy went into me when I was born, and that's why we are connected.

Down the Generations

Letter from One Young Mum to Another

Surrounded by an eerie silence, I lay alone in the bed, scared, so very scared of the choice I had made and what lay ahead. No arm to hold, no hand to squeeze, no reassuring face to help me through the pain of waiting…waiting for dawn to break and wondering if this would finally be the day we would meet.

As night began to leave, you arrived, and I looked at you, one child to another, not knowing what to do or how. But it didn't matter, for now you were mine, and mine alone. When I held your flesh to mine, you melted into my heart and there you have always stayed. When your heart breaks, so too does mine. When your heart trembles, so too does mine. And when your heart jumps for joy, so too does mine.

We are connected.

Looking back on the journey from that day till now, there is still sadness, knowing that life has not treated you fairly, but there is also so much joy in remembering your many triumphs. You have become a remarkable individual, a steadfast sister, a true friend and a brilliant mum.

It is with this knowledge that I can say the choice I made so many years ago was the right one, not just for me, but for everyone else who has walked beside you. You have lived as I have lived, loved as I have loved. Your journey is my journey.

I Always Wanted to be a Mum

I always wanted to be a mum. I come from a large family, and always tried taking over the mother role of my own mum.

I found the man of my dreams and everything was going well. I found out I was pregnant, but unfortunately I had a miscarriage. I fell pregnant again, but I didn't want to believe it was true. Then suddenly I felt a kick. I took a pregnancy test on my partner's birthday and it was positive. My partner and I couldn't believe it.

When I was twenty-six weeks pregnant I had to go to hospital as I had protein in my urine. The midwife said I had signs of pre-eclampsia. At thirty weeks pregnant the doctor took me down for a scan and said I needed to have an emergency caesarean. I was absolutely terrified. My caesarean was the strangest feeling in the world: I giggled throughout the whole operation, it was amazing.

My daughter was rushed to NICU, so I didn't get a chance to see or even hold her. When I finally was able to do so, she fitted in my hand. She was so tiny and only weighed 2lb 5oz.

My daughter changed my life and made it the best. Every day, she is the one that always puts a smile on my face.

I was the second eldest of nine children. My mum was amazing at protecting us and bringing us up. We all had a hard life, but at the age of ten, the man that made our life hard died and then life perked up.

Me and my mum were always very close whilst I was growing up, but we were so alike and often clashed. When I became a teenager, my mum was like my best friend. She was always there if I had anything on my mind or if I needed a shoulder to cry on. I loved helping my mum with my siblings. I felt that she needed a helping hand, and I used to always try and take on the mothering role. My mum is my rock, my best friend and the best mother I could ask for.

My mum is a very caring and loving woman. She puts everyone before herself and has done since she became a mother. My mum was very over-protective of all us children.

When I had a miscarriage, I found it hard to tell her about it. I had no one there for me and it was hard. When I found out I was pregnant again I took a long time to get the courage to tell her, I don't know why. When I eventually told her I was having her first granddaughter she was over the moon. She helped me throughout my pregnancy and was very supportive all the time. When I found out I was going down to have a caesarean, my mum was the first person to arrive at hospital and she was all I wanted apart from my daughter's dad.

After I had my daughter we became closer than ever, and she became protective over her first grandchild too. My mum is my world. I would not know what to do if I lost her.

My New Forever

At the age of twenty I dossed about in a call centre, loved to party, and was in passionate love with my boyfriend. When I announced my pregnancy, instead of cheers of joy, friends didn't know what to say. My pregnancy was peaceful, but I was so scared at the prospect of motherhood. I doubted myself.

Before our little gummy bear was born, I'd never held a baby before. That first night I remember looking at her, and it felt like I was staring at a universe that never ends: what was ahead of me was something vast, but I knew I wasn't able to comprehend the complexity of it all. That night I knew this was my new forever. It was profound.

The first few months were lonely. I was too scared to leave the house, as I didn't have the confidence to breastfeed in public, and I was ashamed of people viewing me as a young mum. I ditched my low-slung baggy jeans and backpacks and reinvented myself in floral dresses and handbags. I didn't sell out on my personal style, I am still the same girl, but my life has diversified.

My mum is my best friend, my light. The more I become a mother, the more I realise how blessed my upbringing was. As each year another birthday passes, I give thanks to the lady who bore me to this world. Growing up I was a typical daddy's girl. I never doubted her love or support whilst growing up, but she was the bad cop and my dad the good cop. Mum was never as tactile as my dad, nor as fun. Now I understand she was the unsung hero of my childhood, always busy backstage, whilst I was having a ball in the forefront with dad. I am embarrassed about my teenage years.

I was scared to tell her I was pregnant and took three separate days off work, as twice I bottled it. I thought she'd be furious. But I will always remember her split-second smile, just before the lecture came tumbling down.

Baby blues second time round, were even lower than the first. She came around after I had been crying and at first asked if I had a cold, to which I responded with a wailing cry. I never cry in front of my mum. She hugged me and told me she loved me and was proud. She's not tactile, but I have never doubted her love. These moments I cherish.

I spent my years growing up thinking my mum was always on my back, to finally understanding she was one of the few who always had my back. From the support my mum has given me with my two children, it makes my heart hurt to know she had three children whilst her family were halfway across the world in Indonesia. I'm pleased she can teach my children about the culture, religion and language.

As my mum was strict with me, I think she has enjoyed being able to treat the girls to desserts and going to bed late – things that just don't happen that often under my watch. Being a grandma is her time to enjoy being the fun one, the silly one, and the tactile one. I secretly smile when I hear myself giving my eldest girl, now four, the exact same tellings off my mum gave me. And I am happily a self-proclaimed bad cop. As I tell my boyfriend, I didn't give birth so I could have another mate. I am here to raise and prepare them for the world. But with that, there will be laughter, love, nonsense and fun.

She Helped Me Become the Parent I am Today

I was seventeen when I had my first son. After five days of slow labour he was finally born on the Sunday weighing 7lb 4oz, only fitting into tiny baby clothes. When I left the hospital my journey of being a young mum would began: and I knew it would be the hardest thing I would ever do.

Being twenty-three now with two sons is a challenge. I found I was pregnant with my second son on Father's Day. There were lots of changes coming our way: we had just signed for our new home and I was expecting a new baby. At forty weeks I was told that my baby had a bad heart. I only had three days to prepare myself. He was due on a Thursday and born on the Saturday, weighing 7lb 3oz and fighting fit. On the Sunday he was rushed to NICU covered in wires to have his heart monitored. It was the worst thing, seeing my tiny baby in all these wires.

My mum had four children, three girls and one boy, me being the middle child. My mum is a nanny to three grandsons and one granddaughter. My mum raised me with my stepdad after my alcoholic dad left when I was two years of age, and he hasn't ever bothered since. But we had an amazing upbringing. We never went without. My mum and stepdad were hard-working parents and went on to take a foster child on. They showed us the meaning of a family.

As a child, myself and my mum didn't have the strongest relationship: it was pretty rocky. Now being an adult with my own children, me and my mum have the strongest relationship. She was my rock through both my pregnancies and giving birth to my boys. I rely on my mum for everything. She comes to every hospital appointment with my youngest son so we both understand my little boy's conditions. She helped me become the parent I am today. She's an amazing nanny to both my boys and loves spoiling them.

I Miss How Our Relationship Used to Be

From a young age I knew I wanted to be a mum, once I had my own house and a lifetime supportive partner. However, it didn't quite work out the way I imagined. I had my daughter at seventeen, whilst still living at my mother's house. My daughter's father then left me when she was just four months old and has never contacted us since. She is now three years old.

Although things didn't go the way I wanted them to, within the three years of being a mum I now have my own house, my daughter has the best stepdaddy in the world, and we are expecting our second child together!

I am the youngest of three children. When I was younger, I always thought my mum was the best mum in the world. I thought this even though she was always distracted by men, always putting them before me and my brothers. I didn't understand why my brothers were never that close to her. Since having my daughter, I have realised that the way she treated us as children was wrong. I will never put my daughter through the things she let us go through and see. I am determined to give my daughter the best possible life: she deserves it.

My mother is genuinely loving and caring towards my daughter and enjoys being her nanna. She always likes to be supportive in my child's life. Though our bond isn't as strong as it was when I was my daughter's age, my daughter loves my mum, so that's all that matters to me.

Ebb and Flow

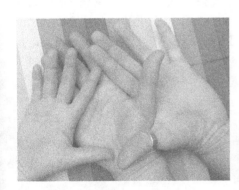

Sometimes close and connected, sometimes distant. There is an expectation of a mother's love being consistent. We hope that it will flow smoothly and dependably. But what is it like when this isn't the case? What happens when the love and sense of connection is in flux: there at times and not at others?

There are women who spend their lives moving in and out of connection with their mothers. It is not a stable ground. There is love, joy and laughter there, for some women there is a deep affection, but it is not always easy to reach. There can be an ambivalence to the relationship that may continue after the daughter herself becomes a mother.

These are tricky waters to navigate. Women who experience this 'ebb and flow' relationship with their mothers talk about wanting to be more steady and consistent for their own children. There is a strong desire to create stability and security.

No Space to Breathe

For as long as I can remember 'motherhood' has occupied a fraught space for me. At school I spent lunchtimes making maternal figures out of clay. I spent the next decade or more thinking about motherhood as a way of approaching lots of stuff. All the time, though, I knew that I didn't want to be a mother myself.

When did I transition to motherhood? The moment I read the cheap pregnancy test? The first scan? The first kick? The first signs of labour? First cries?

The ambivalence about motherhood I have always felt has strengthened since I became a mum. Though it was only nine months ago, I cannot remember the first few weeks and months of motherhood. To function as a mother, and a mother who works full-time, has involved a forgetting of what it has taken to get here. But it is a forgetting visible in my skin and bones, marked with the traces and aches of pregnancy, labour and those exhausted weeks and months. The challenge for me is to acknowledge and find a language to speak about how the irrevocable physical, emotional and temporal changes align with my working identity, which hasn't changed much.

I remember she wrote me a letter once about how she never wanted to be a mum. It was not that she didn't want us, but she didn't want the prison life that being a mum at that time meant. She couldn't breathe.

I always felt there was no space between us. There was no space to breathe. So much of what I remember of my childhood is me trying to separate, me trying to make space. I also remember play, colour, wool, books…I remember absolute generosity; moods and vulnerabilities; pain and laughter; food and no food. Perhaps our relationship had always turned on its axis and part of my daughterhood has been caring and holding responsibility.

My mother died when I was eight weeks pregnant. It is hard to write about her death and harder still about a death and a life that are somehow socially unacceptable. Because she was more than how she died, and more than the parts of herself that were painful. And although we didn't have a relationship that looked like most mothers and daughters, we had our relationship. My mother is my muse. The gifts she gave me were a fierce belief in the truth: that people, things, relationships are more complicated than they look, and how, with a little bravery, you can find the art and the beauty in the ugliest of things.

My mother left the country when I was nineteen or twenty. She went back to find the home that was taken from her as a child (she was a child refugee). In one sense, we never really had the opportunity to know what we could be like when we both grew up.

The last conversation I can remember really having with my mum was about how there are no tights that don't fall down. We both laughed and she said the only way was to wear knickers over the top. This sums up our relationship as adults: intimate, inane and full of humour.

I know that my mother worked hard not to repeat the abuse that she experienced from her own mother. Part of my learning to be a mother is learning how to remember the joys, freedoms and love that my mother gave me and repeat these quiet acts of love and security.

One thing I would like as a mother is to be a stable ground for my daughter. And I want us both to have space between us. Me and my mum were many things, but as a child and a teenager it was hard for us to talk and hear each other. I want to be a better ear for my daughter. And I would like to be a bit braver.

I Want to be More Solid

I used a donor, who is a lovely, generous man, after years of searching. I had the unshakeable support of my partner, family and friends. It was a great pregnancy and I gave birth at home in a pool. This was closely followed by very anxious days in hospital due to my baby having a suspected serious infection.

Despite the support that I had, I felt isolated: adjusting to being on my own with my daughter a lot and awake often throughout the night. I needed more time from my mum than she gave, though I didn't ever tell her this.

I was amazed by my baby and that I had carried her safely all the way through. She is such a gift to me and my partner. The challenge that I have is that I struggle to relax and just be. I find it hard to be still and quiet, and I miss the company of other adults. I'm easily distracted and want to feel more solid for my child. My mood shifts, it's changeable but I strive to be calmer within myself, and less reactive to worry and to feeling provoked.

As a young person, I sought guidance and support from older women outside of my family, as it wasn't straightforward with my mum and dad. Mum was always carrying a lot as she had three children and a husband who struggled, I believe, with himself and in his role as church leader. It wasn't steady at home and my parents were loving but temperamental. I remember my mum's disappointment, her expressing that when I was teenager; feeling like there were a lot of expectations of me that I could not fulfil. I argued a lot with my parents. I grew up being told that if I believed in God and followed his word,

I would have eternal life in heaven. When I came out, we grew closer and our relationship shifted, but still there is an enormous barrier there.

I feel even more connected to my mum through my journey to being a parent, and that continues. I feel her love for us deeply. My mum and dad were both quite stressed and now I am too. We don't see my parents as often as any of us would like. When we're all together, my mum is very involved with my daughter, who follows her everywhere. But she has also started pushing at the cracks in my relationship with my parents, testing the existing conflict areas.

Barren Mother Seeks Baby

When a mother is missing her baby, there is loss: gaping-mouthed, a paused, hollow O. A cavernous trunk roots deep into Mother Earth…but where is her baby?

I honestly believe I wished my baby into being.

I had to chant my daughter into life. I closed my eyes and felt her there, on me, breathing a rhythm, exhaling hope and gratitude for being.

When we first see our baby, she's wearing someone else's baby clothes: a knitted, pink hat and white, bobbly baby-gro, donated to the hospital. They don't want to clothe her. It's too painful.

I claim her and wrap her like a shellfish in a woollen blanket. When the birth parents come back, we exchange gifts. I offer tea in the hospital room as if I am a host. We sit around the birthing bed, feeding our shared new baby and talk for a long time together about dogs we've rescued and re-homed in the past.

When it happens, it is swift. It's a ceremonial exchange. Time pauses, a space opens and we quickly step in, awaiting our cue, no time to rehearse. Someone certificates. Everyone's lives have taken a different track. We are all now cast together in this act.

We ground ourselves with chitter-chatter and search around to find other things to connect us together. Really, it is only this monumental act. We all know our roles are to be recorded. History can trace us easily.

I switch relief for gratitude. I say goodbye to my fertility thermometer. I say goodbye to needing and hoping. I am saying goodbye because I am healed. I am not just a mother. I am her mother. I am paired. We are in binary with each other. I am, because of her and she is, because of me.

My mother was a young mother at seventeen. I was her second baby at nineteen. As a Catholic, she struggles with intimacy and was ashamed of anything associated with the body or sexuality. When I came out as a lesbian, her disgust was visceral. She doesn't engage in anything intimate, so she has never accepted me and my sexuality. She pretends to. But I can feel it. She is transactional and sometimes gets emotional and I can connect with her, but it is intermittent. Our attachment is therefore inconsistent and goes in and out of frequency. I work very hard not to pass that disengagement on to my daughter. I have forced myself to learn how to be intimate and love my body so that I can teach my child how to live with intimacy.

I have good memories of my mother. She seemed really caring and loved me through provision of food. She used to bake, make cakes, she made me cheese and onion pie with her own pastry. She made and sent me food packages when I was at university.

The relationship changed when I came out at about twenty-four. My dad is very aggressive, and I think she felt she had to choose between me and her marriage. She chose him.

Before I came out, I became pregnant on a one-night stand and I knew I could never tell her. So I went to my friend's mum, who helped me, but made me swear an oath that I would never tell my mother that she helped me get an abortion. I never have told my mum, over twenty-five years later.

I pierced my nose after that traumatic event and my parents were so furious that they decided to stop funding my rent at university. Everything seems to spring back to this conflict. Whenever I confide in her something intimate or painful, my mother thinks I want something from her and is disappointed all over again.

I have tried hard to reduce the impact of my parenting on my child. My mother adores my child, but her priority is her life and my dad. My mother changes her plans all the time, which is disorientating. I can see flashes of the disappointment I must have felt as a small child, in my own daughter when this happens.

My mother has quite fixed ideas about gender roles and so buys my daughter things that are pink and have rabbits and princesses on them. I avoid these stereotypes. My daughter, of course, loves them.

My mother seems to have amnesia about how hard it is to parent a child, and takes some pleasure in seeing me tired and in a life of drudgery. She compares it to her life, and I think she wants it to be just as hard as hers was.

I hope I am able to make my daughter's life experience better through being on her side and helping and supporting her. I am trying to be myself with my child, to be in the moment so I can grow with her and remain connected with her. I work hard to sustain the connection.

When my baby was born, I enjoyed my mother and my grandmother staying with us for a while and connecting with them. My grandmothers were the best people in my life and I often felt closer to them than I did to my mother. Now I can see my mum is carving out a similar role. My daughter is very like my mum. They have the same taste in things already. My daughter is born a week in-between her two grandmothers' birthdays. More and more, my daughter likes to connect with her grandparents without me there.

Roots to Grow and Wings to Fly

When I found out I was pregnant with my daughter it was the second time I had been pregnant. I was shocked: it was unplanned, the dad and I weren't together at the time due to his controlling and jealous nature. Would it work? Could I be mother to this baby?

We went back and forth, yes to no, excited to scared, lovers to haters, blaming and wanting to make the right decision. Together, not together. Crying and planning. I was unsure, but thought I might not get another chance. Once I saw her on the scan and I felt her move inside me, I knew I wanted to have her. My protective maternal instincts kicked in and I decided to proceed.

The pregnancy was uncomfortable for all of the above reasons and many more. I had planned a natural home birth, but on the fifteenth day after the due date my baby decided she was coming out. After twenty hours of pain, being rushed to the hospital and an emergency C-section, she was born. Unfortunately, they had given me so much spinal block I couldn't hold her when she came out, so our bonding didn't take place until much later.

Mum had a couple of major secrets that affected me, which I didn't know about until my dad blurted them out in an argument. Trust and stability were extinguished in a downpour of emotions. Our relationship before that had been interesting. I was her favourite and would often comfort her when she was unhappy, which seemed to be a lot of the time. Through my twenties we grew apart as I tried to make sense of the revelations. One really low point in my life became the turning point where I faced up to it all and accepted what was. Not long after this my baby was born, and my mum was a huge strength and support to me. I have valued my mum so much more since becoming a mother myself and our relationship continues to grow with life's ebb and flow.

My mum plays a lovely, caring part in my child's life and has always been supportive. I don't often ask her for advice, but I know she's there. My relationship with my child is interesting: fierce, turbulent but ultimately very close and loving. She has traits of both myself and her father, which are a delight and challenge in equal measure. Seeing your child grow into their own person is an honour and a wonder, but hard when they make their mistakes. We give them roots to grow and wings to fly – that's the theory.

A Re-Working Kind of Time

I was shocked at my response to pregnancy on both a physical and emotional level. My parents were shocked at my experience and I felt they couldn't contain my anxiety. I was nauseous for the first half of pregnancy and deeply disturbed by my body when I felt the hardening in my tummy. I wasn't able to touch or look at it for two weeks.

My pregnancy was planned and wanted, and the image people had of me was along the earth mother lines. Instead, I was pretty anxious, and it challenged my sense of self massively. I felt my gender and presentation (female/femme) was challenged. As a queer woman (bisexual) in a relationship with a man I felt really confused by our roles and the expectations on us from others, ourselves and societal norms. I am still deciphering the roles that gender and sexuality have had in my transition to parenthood.

I have had such incredible support from my partner, and I feel we are both in it one hundred percent. He has made me breakfast and a cup of tea every day since she was born. She is now six months old. I love my baby and partner so much and I feel loved by them, but it's taken six months to get to say this so freely.

My mum looked after me, my sister and brother while my dad worked away a lot. She did an amazing job on her own, but it impacted her and us. I don't remember closeness but I am told it was there. Strangely, this surprises me, perhaps as I am still processing the bits where she was emotionally absent. My mum's way of coping with trauma was to close down. She still uses this coping mechanism, although I feel her trying to connect and learn from things I bring to her attention.

I remember her tummy and loving it. I felt like it was a lovely squidgy thing that I came from. It made me feel safe. In later life she had a tummy tuck. I was deeply disturbed by this and felt it had wounded something very important to me.

My mum mothered her own mother and her siblings and had to bear great responsibility. She is now mothering her mother again while she deteriorates in a care home. I feel love from her, and she is always there for me, but not always emotionally available on the level I need. This is an ongoing negotiation for us.

Throughout pregnancy and the last six months of mothering my baby, I have taken to looking back at the young me and my experiences, as well as at my mum's experience of mothering me and of being mothered herself. It's been a funny kind of circle, a re-working kind of time. My mother and I are learning how to shift our relationship from one where she knows best, to more of a discussion. I am sad about how I was left to cry (very normal for her generation). She is learning from me about current parenting thinking.

My mum is learning how to be a granny and she is engaged and lovely with my baby. I want to work, whereas my mum didn't get that chance. I want to protect my baby from gendered norms as much as possible. I want her to feel free to be whoever she discovers she is.

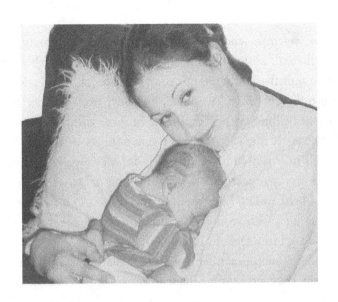

Barriers

Love, warmth, cuddles – these are things we closely associate with being 'mothered'. Human babies are programmed to attach to their mothers. After nine months in the womb they need touch, protection, nourishment and warmth. Oxytocin,[‡] we hope, will flow from mother to child and child to mother, filling both with a sense of love, safety and security. The more positive touch there is, the more this bond is increased. Responding to these needs may not come instinctively for all mothers. Various factors including birth trauma, postnatal depression, external stressors, and not having herself been held and cuddled as an infant, can affect a mother's ability to attach to her child. With so much expectation on mothers to bond with their child, there are often feelings of failure that accompany such challenges.

One woman describes feeling that there was a barrier between herself and her mother, preventing them from getting too close. Another sees that her mother's social repression is behind her inability to show affection. Other women talk about something missing, a 'lack', a coldness that has passed down from one generation to the next. It is as though the two bodies of mother and child, that we imagine will be lovingly and closely connected, are instead walled off from one another.

Mothers who have experienced such coldness are often determined to be warmer and more openly affectionate with their own children. When they themselves give birth, and look for their mother's care and support, they may find that again it is lacking. However, there can be another transition that takes place. In some cases, the grandmother is able to connect with her grandchildren in a warmer, more affectionate way. It is as though she is given a second chance to love, through this new generation once removed. Perhaps grandchildren can find new ways to break through the barriers; perhaps having the distance of a generation and less pressure directly on herself, allows the grandmother to be more openly loving.

....

‡ Oxytocin is sometimes known as the 'love hormone'. It is released into the bloodstream in response to stretching of the cervix and uterus during labour, with stimulation of the nipples from breastfeeding and with positive touch. It helps with birth, bonding, attachment, trust, social interaction and milk production.

I Want my Daughter to be Free

I became a mother at what felt like the eleventh hour. I was forty and hadn't been with my partner for that long when we conceived. Before I met this partner, I had truly faced up to the idea of having no child. It was a bizarrely content moment. I was single, free and really liked myself. And my sadness was uncomplicated. Then I fell in love, head over heels and slightly bonkers. My breeding impetus went into overdrive. After two weeks I told him he was the daddy, and so it was. I knew I was pregnant the moment we conceived, literally, we both did. Just looked at each other and said, "Oh my God!" That pregnancy lasted eight weeks. It was beautiful and sad. I was so grateful to have had the experience of pregnancy, whatever happened next. What did happen next was an even more heightened desire to be pregnant again. This time I had the most incredible full pregnancy. Never have I felt so empowered and energised, so natural, so instinctive.

My mum is a lovely woman. But she was terribly repressed as a child, growing up with authoritative parents in middle-class Surrey in the 1950s. She chose a kind of repressing husband in my dad, and her stifled nature was of course passed on to me. She did her best, but I have a sense of never having fully been allowed to stretch my wings, to allow my wildness out. I felt boxed in, with too much emphasis placed on what others thought. I believe she's really a poet, a hippy and a radical. But those things aren't allowed in our family culture, and I hide those sides of myself from her.

As a child she said that she knew what I was thinking. I knew that was true, and I knew what she was thinking too. Now that bond doesn't exist. She has shut down something and I'm not brave enough to open it up. There's also no need. She's actually kind of happy just as she is and doesn't need me opening up a can of worms in her seventies. I'm, however, left with the restrictions I impose on myself, embedded by my upbringing. She was kind, she was good, and she never rocked any boats.

I think, in some ways, having a daughter has brought my mother and I a bit closer. Subtly. My daughter has worn some 1940s baby dresses that Mum wore and I wore. I had a wonderful feeling when I did up the buttons, of a lineage of women. But our basic relationship hasn't changed.

I love the relationship my daughter has with her grandma. She totally loves her, and fantastically breaks through awkward physical barriers by just clambering on her lap and cuddling her. Most unlike my family!

I am parenting in a very consciously different way and trying to undo the repression. But I am scared that I can't. I have found myself tutting and sighing lately at my daughter's three-year-old behaviour: those not-so-subtle messages I grew up with of being somehow unacceptable. There's an anger and a volatility in my relationship with my daughter that flares up sometimes. I don't know how to deal with it, as I have no precedent, and anger is a scary emotion to those who grew up with it as taboo. I'd really like to change that. I want my daughter to be free to be angry, passionate, joyful, wild, miserable, boring, exciting, without it affecting her own sense of self-worth. And I guess I'd like that for myself too.

An Absence, A Void

I felt very grounded in my pregnancies and enjoyed the physical experience. I thought I had prepared for my first birth, but the reality was a big shock. I found the intensity and frequency of the pain traumatic, and never got into the pool in our front room where I had thought I would give birth. The first few days were even more shocking: I felt full of love for my baby, but bowled over by the emotional and physical changes, and lack of sleep. I thought my partner and I would cope fine with a new baby, but in reality we needed a lot more support. I was completely overwhelmed. My world turned upside down, I was so determined to be a good mother to this new child that all my focus turned on trying to fulfil that role, neglecting both myself and my relationship with my partner.

With my second pregnancy and birth I made sure I got a lot more support, and subsequently the birth and first weeks were a much gentler experience. Being a mum challenges me daily, but I love it too. The relationship between my children is a real joy to observe.

My mother had postnatal depression after having me, for which there was not a lot of help or understanding at the time. I think this early period, and the lack of support that she had, affected our attachment. I do remember sometimes feeling close as I grew up, but mostly there is a kind of void where feelings of attachment could be. She was there throughout my life until I left home, but also somehow not there. I remember her being very unhappy at times, and at others emotionally removed, she seemed frustrated and unfulfilled. Then again, I remember her singing to me at night when I could not sleep and holding me on her lap to eat soup when I was poorly.

During my pregnancies and after the births of my children, I felt this aching gap where there could have been a woman – a mother – I could lean back into. But instead there was an absence, a void, a great pain and sense of loss. There was no one to call and ask for advice, no one to interfere and tell me how to do things, no one to offer guidance and wisdom, no older woman to look at my children with the same inherited, blood-line of love I feel for them.

Becoming a mum has helped me understand how tough and exhausting mothering day after day can be, and I have much more empathy for my mother. However, it also made me realise how much I love my children, how much I would do for them, and emphasised my sense of not having been brought up in a nurturing, affectionate environment. I am so determined to do things differently, that I fall into all sorts of other problems. I frequently don't get it right, but I always make sure that I'm there, that I apologise to my children if I get things wrong and that they know, and feel, how loved they are each and every day. I also do find myself doing some things the same, such as singing songs my mum sang to me. These things make me realise how strong that connection is, even when you no longer see each other.

There...but Sometimes Sort of Not

I trained as a children's nurse and got married as soon as my training finished. I wanted children of my own and was very sad when my first pregnancy miscarried. The first months of my second pregnancy were filled with anxiety, but all was well and I bloomed with health. I loved being pregnant.

My daughter was born after a normal labour. I had held hundreds of other women's babies, but holding my own was completely different. I felt such love, but also fear at the responsibility. Those first months were a roller-coaster.

My son arrived three years later, after another healthy pregnancy. The biggest challenges of motherhood came in my son's teenage years. I lost touch with him. I became depressed and couldn't manage his difficult behaviour. What had happened to my little boy? It was the most painful time of my life.

My mum was there... but sometimes she sort of wasn't. I know now that was because she was anxious and depressed. I loved her but was afraid of her. I had to make sure that I was a good girl, so that I didn't do the wrong thing and make her angry.

I knew that her childhood had been a sad one. Her mum died when she was four years old, and her older sister, just a child herself, had been left to look after her and her twin sister. It was tough. I knew I was lucky to have a mum.

We lived with my dad's mum and I was close to my grandmother who I called mother. My mum didn't like my grandmother. I can see now how difficult it was for her to live in a small house with her husband's widowed mother. My mum didn't play with us. I don't remember her singing to us or cuddling us. Life seemed to just be hard work for my mum. She was hard on herself, and on my sister and I.

My relationship with my mother was difficult. I wanted to be close to her, but it was as though we both had this barrier stopping us from getting too close. My mum mellowed in middle age, and our relationship did become closer when I had children. She was more loving as a grandma than she was as a mother and my children loved her. I was very, very conscious of the wish to not be the cold mother that my mum had been, and I vowed to not hit my children because I was angry. I did find myself acting in ways that my mum had. It was difficult to break the patterns that were deeply ingrained in me, but I was determined.

When the relationship with my son broke down, I sought professional help. My mum would never have done that. When my mum got dementia, all the pain and anger of both her childhood and mine erupted like a volcano. I never made peace with her, which makes me sad.

I am a grandmother now and it's a joy to spend time with my granddaughters. It is probably the reaching of maturity, but since having grandchildren, I have a deeper understanding and compassion for my mum, my daughter and for myself.

I Felt this Absence Deeply

From a very young age I knew I wanted to be a mum. When I was about to get married, I was told I had endometriosis and that I might not be able to have children. We decided to try for a baby as soon as we got married. When my period didn't come on its due date, I took a test that day…and the next… and the next. Eventually I believed the three positives!

My due date came and went and, although we tried everything, the pregnancy just went on. At forty-two weeks I was scanned and the medical team decided to induce my labour. The labour was very hard and very painful but relatively fast for a first baby. I was given a lot of pain relief and felt very out of control. My labour ended in my son being born after a lot of panic due to shoulder dystocia. I saw that my baby was very blue and nobody spoke: I thought he was dead. I looked to see what it was and thought, "Oh I had a boy, but he's dead now." Eventually I realised he wasn't dead as they whisked him away and gave him some oxygen and got him crying.

I didn't feel the immediate burst of love some mothers describe, I actually remember thinking, "I've gone through all this and now I don't want this baby." But I carried on going through the motions. Twenty-four hours after he was born, I was still in hospital and I had been feeding him hourly. I looked down at him and thought, "He's quite sweet." Our love grew from there, I think.

My mother is a doctor and when I was a child she often worked in the evenings as well as during the day. I felt this absence deeply. I think this is part of the reason that I was determined that I would be at home for my children. My father was at home with us, but I felt that a lot of the time he was distracted and wanting to do other things. My parents did not work well together, and it was easy to play one off against the other. After my sister died, I felt very cross with my mother: she was the one person who could have warned me of what was coming and she didn't even when I asked her. She was, and still is, very much a follower of the man in her life (my dad when I was a child and my stepfather now). I think she was a much nicer mother to me when she was alone with me or in-between her relationships.

Mostly my mum has a very good relationship with my children. They adore her and love going to her house and spending time with her. She spends time playing with them and gives them good attention. I don't really spend much quality time with my mother, we tend to pass each other when handing the children over. I feel determined to be there for my kids and to show them that being themselves is good and okay. I try to laugh with them as much as I can, and I tell them I love them all of the time. I don't really remember my mum telling me she loved me very much at all. I was so determined to do nothing the way my parents did, and this led me to do the opposite, which maybe didn't allow me to discover what was really the right way for me.

The Empty Frame

From the moment of the birth of my first child, motherhood for me has been difficult. The pushing part of the birth was long: I didn't know what I was doing, and I was tied down by intravenous infusions.

My daughter was very wanted and planned. Myself and my husband were happily married and had been together since we were seventeen. I think it was these deep roots that enabled us to survive becoming parents. For the first year things were hell. I felt rubbish about my appearance, having gained lots of weight in pregnancy. I resented everyone and everything. I had no useful support from anyone other than my husband. Looking back, I can see I was depressed, but in the haze of the first year I could not see the wood for the trees. My husband put up with so much: I was really horrible to him. I hated him for no good reason. The reality was I hated what being a mum had done to my carefree life.

Things didn't improve until my husband finally snapped back at me a year after her birth. Slowly things began to improve, but I felt lost for a very, very long time. With distance from those early days I can see clearer. Now I feel that becoming a mum resulted in the death of who I was. The empty frame of my new life started from the moment I became a mum.

When I think of my mother when I was young, I think of her always busy with housework: the house was exceptionally clean and tidy. She never really had friends and never socialised, she was miserable most of the time. I never remember her sitting on the floor playing with me or my siblings, she was always too busy. But I do remember having a laugh with her in my older years.

It's clear why my mother is so cold: her mother was exactly the same. It's my biggest fear that I will be that way with my own children, though I try my best to avoid it. I always make sure I tell my children I love them, as I don't ever remember my mother telling me. She does now but rarely. She lives just five minutes away from me and has done the whole time I have been a mother. She will babysit if I ask, but always makes me feel bad for asking. I see her probably once a month.

Being a mother has really exposed my flaws as a person. I want to be the best parent I can, but often feel a failure. I didn't see it for a long time, but I often use housework to avoid having to spend time with the kids when it's all been too much, just as my mother did.

My daughter is a handful and I find it difficult at times. I'm really disappointed by how little involvement my mother has in my children's lives and how little support I get. The positive thing about this is that my relationship with my husband is stronger than ever. We work hard to spend quality time with the children and parent them differently to how I was parented. The experience of loving a little person unconditionally is the best thing I have in my life.

With Fresh Eyes

I'm lucky that I have a wonderful husband who has always been there for me. We've been together since school and we always wanted a big family.

My first pregnancy was amazing, I enjoyed every bit of it. But birth was hard. We started our birthing journey at home in a birth pool, but after a long and exhausting pre-labour we ended up in hospital and after a few hours of pushing I held my baby in my arms. She was a miracle. At first, I did not know what to do, or what I was supposed to feel. She was so strong and fragile at the same time.

When my second child was born, I was much more aware and confident, so birth and parenting seemed a bit easier. I learned a lot about trust, belief and love from my children. It's hard being a thousand miles away from my family, but I just learned to live my life like that. Three years after my son was born, I gave birth to the most beautiful little girl. She makes me laugh and gives me strength to believe in myself and my feelings, and to carry on doing things my own way.

I'm one of three children, a middle child. I grew up in my family feeling left out and being different. I have few memories from my childhood and none about my mum reading me stories or cuddling me. I never felt loved or supported. What I do remember is feeling ashamed, foolish and sad.

My relationship with my mum got even worse during my teenage years. When I went to college I started to be more independent, I started seeing things differently than in our house. I learned that life could be more fun. I learned to express my feelings, to talk and to listen. My mum did not like this, so I spent less time at home, and we did not communicate much.

In my adult life I could avoid being in touch with my mum. I left my home country seven years ago, leaving behind my parents and my past. But when I had my first child, suddenly grandparents became important and I wanted my child to have a connection with her family. They were excited too as she was their first grandchild. But my mum never supported me, she never showed any sign that she thinks I'm good enough as a mother or that I'm capable of being responsible or caring for someone.

My daughter was a high-need child. I used to carry her all the time in a sling, I could not put her down for five minutes and she would not sleep any longer than half an hour. So, by the time she was one I was absolutely worn-out. My mother kept telling me what I was doing wrong and how I should leave my baby to cry.

As I get older and experience life as a parent, I have started seeing my relationship with my mum differently. I am not angry about her anymore. I'd like to understand the reasons why she didn't listen to me or my siblings, and why she can't accept my personality as it is. I believe that if I keep searching for these answers, I will be able to see her with fresh eyes. My main task now is to be a 'good enough' mum. I want my children to feel safe, secure and loved for who they are. I want them to know that I will be there for them with all my heart as long as I can.

Fracture Lines

Sometimes things go wrong – badly wrong – leaving fracture lines in our lives and relationships. Childhood trauma can wreak havoc on a child's sense of identity and their ongoing relationships with others. Pivotal to recovery is how the trauma is dealt with. If the experience is recognised and the child supported in their responses to the trauma, the fractures can begin to be processed and healed. If the experience is negated or repressed by adults in the child's life, the fracture lines burrow deep underground. Over time these can become deep fissures.

Where a mother has been unable to protect her daughter, or has inflicted harm upon her, the daughter can be left without a solid, safe point of attachment. Becoming mothers themselves, these women talk about lacking 'a compass' and feeling that their mothering is 'not good enough'. They have learnt how important it is for their own children to have a strong point of attachment, but how do they provide this? There can be a friction between wanting to meet their child's needs and not having had their own needs met whilst growing up; trying to provide solid ground, whilst not being fully rooted themselves.

It is interesting to note that some of the women with younger children appear to be immersed in this struggle, whereas those whose children are older or grown up, recognise that they have been 'good enough mothers' and continue to have good relationship with their children. Maybe the fact that they have become aware of what they have lacked, reflected on this and tried to do something new, makes all the difference. The fractures can't simply be eradicated or denied, but they can be witnessed and prevented from running through the new relationship of mother and child.

Here the grandmother, mother, child triptych is especially problematic. The central woman can struggle to know how to relate both backwards and forwards at the same time. If her mother remains in denial of the trauma, is it possible for her to be part of her grandchildren's lives? For many women this is an ongoing negotiation.

An Absence of Consciousness

By the time my husband and I agreed to try for a family I was thirty-six years old. We struggled to conceive. But then, as a result of an IUI procedure, I fell pregnant with twins. We were elated! Unfortunately, the twins' hearts stopped beating in the first trimester. I was beyond devastated. A long scream came from my body and it felt like it would never stop.

All I wanted to do was get pregnant again as soon as possible, and by January I was pregnant with my son. I tried to hold on to him. I wrote him a journal, I sang to him. "Please stay," I would whisper to him, holding my belly. And he did. He is wonderful.

I struggle to be grateful. I really struggle with the intensity of motherhood. I put myself under a ton of pressure, trying to undo my own experience of being a child.

My mother is an addict and chronic alcoholic. I spent a lot of my childhood overcome with fear, it swirled inside my stomach constantly and distracted me from my heart and the heart of others. I slowly went numb.

I loved my mother so very much, but she was very distracted by her illness, and there were many things she didn't see. In her absence of consciousness, I was sexually abused. But on a much deeper level, I was overlooked and grew up with great longing. She was loving, kind and cuddly, but not consistently so. I think she is a lovely narcissist, if there can be such a thing.

My mother got sober and stayed sober for some time when I was twelve. It was then that I started to fall apart. My body filled up with black rage that was mostly directed back on myself and at her. We went on like that for a number of years, me being angry and her being sorry. At the age of twenty-three I left New Zealand permanently and never went back. Our painful history sits between us as we muddle along trying to forge a relationship that works.

The way I was mothered has definitely affected the way I mother. I constantly feel I am not giving, being, doing enough. This is how my mother felt about herself, it is how I felt about my own childhood and now I carry it into my mothering. It links all of our experience. I would like to change it if I can.

Since becoming a mother, I have felt both a little more compassionate towards my mother and a little more angry. Being a good mother is such a momentous task, one that is of great value to another little vulnerable human being, and one that requires and deserves great commitment. I still feel my mother could, to this day, come to mothering differently. Mostly I feel pulled between the fear of a closer relationship and the longing for one. I have thought a lot more about her since having my sons. I miss her. I miss having a mum around. If she were sober, I know she would bring me baking, flowers and other little treasures as a wee way of sprinkling love on my life. I think of her every day. I don't know the way forward.

For Now, it Has to Be Like This

My experience of becoming a mother has completely and utterly changed my life. I had many years of abuse from my mother and various relationships. I also experienced numerous sexual assaults whilst vulnerable. Having my daughter has grounded me, given me a reason to live and brought real love into my life. If I hadn't have had her when I did, I truly wonder if I would be here today.

In all honesty I don't have the words to express my gratitude for her. At thirty-six years old I had nothing: a world of broken abusive relationships, unstable work, no money, very little family connection. I had always desperately wanted a baby, but time was ticking away and the stability and means to have one seemed a million miles away. I sought comfort once again in my abusive ex, who was living with his partner and, in a nutshell, he agreed to give me a child. We tried a couple of times and I fell pregnant.

The 'relationship' with my lover broke down when I was pregnant. I was on my own with my daughter. I have struggled so much at times with doing it all mostly on my own. I have struggled with her demands, the relentlessness, managing my moods and hers, but I have always sought the advice and help I need, so I can work to break the patterns from my past, and try to be the best mum I can.

My daughter is four now. She is amazing, strong, confident, witty, clever, so alive and truly beautiful. She makes me laugh every day and I cherish the love I feel for her. I feel so proud of her, sometimes proud of us both!

My mother was emotionally and psychologically abusive and neglected my emotional needs as a child. She is a nurse and she would always seem to show care if I was physically ill but was not there for me emotionally. I believe now that she has narcissistic personality disorder. I experienced sexual abuse in my teens, but she has never shown empathy, care or compassion: much of it was ignored or I was blamed for it. She used me to prop her up and meet her needs. She doesn't understand unconditional love or that as a parent you are there to meet your child's needs and not the other way around.

I'm determined that my daughter will never feel the way I did. No one has ever made me feel as worthless as my own mother. She taught me to hate myself. I am teaching my child to love and cherish herself. I wing it a lot, as I have no compass, but I'm committed to keep trying to heal and grow and accept the best I can.

It seemed so much better to start with when I had my baby. I was glad I got back in contact with my mother, she started to relate to me as an individual. She showed warmth and care towards my little girl and I thought things had really changed. But it didn't last. My daughter was a very challenging three-year-old. I leaned on my mother, sometimes in tears on the phone after struggling with tantrums. My mum started to pathologise her and kept suggesting there might be something wrong her and that she might need a psychologist. It all got very painful and I pulled right back from my mum. I know deep down, and through all the people who know my daughter, that there was nothing wrong with my little girl, other than being a strong-minded, stubborn, feisty three-year-old.

I know it's harsh but I don't trust my mum. I am hoping in time I will relax more and feel less nervous about the way she could be with my daughter, because initially it warmed my heart to see her love for my little girl. I felt that maybe, even on a subconscious level, she was making up for things by being a loving granny. But, for now, it has to be like this.

A Rod for Your Own Back

I knew by the time I was eight years old, that I would not be the same kind of mother to my children that my mother was to me.

Having married the first person that asked me, I had three normal conceptions. My first two pregnancies were straightforward, and I felt amazing despite the sickness. I belonged to an elite group of women who were moving on from the maiden into the mother sphere of life and I truly relished that challenge. I fell pregnant very quickly the third time and, like a ship in full sail, moved month by month through this pregnancy. I had epidural deliveries with my first two as I had 'back labour' which is gruesome. But with my third it was the most beautiful and ecstatic delivery I could have wished for. I only had a little gas and air and felt the exhilaration of the physical changes one's body goes through from bearing down to pushing the baby out, it was positively orgasmic.

My mother married at nineteen, had me at twenty, my brother at twenty-one and my sister at twenty-two. When I was two-and-a-half I was involved in a horrific road accident and almost died. I was in hospital for six months and had to learn how to walk all over again. When my younger sister was born, she was diagnosed with very serious cystic fibrosis. From then, until her premature death aged four, it was a round of one hospital visit after another, either for me or her. When my baby sister died my brother and I were six and five years old and 'shielded' from the whole thing – as was the case in those days. Not until I was fifty-six did my mother and I have a conversation about how that event had impacted on us. My mother said that until that moment, she had never given a thought to how our sister's death had affected us.

Much later in life, with my own children as adults and becoming parents themselves, I have some understanding of why my mother was the way she was. But that does not make up for the years of misery I and my siblings suffered at the hands of both parents until we left home. From the day of my sister's death our parents became emotionally absent from us. As we hit puberty our parents announced the potential arrival of another baby and I suppose I was hopeful that this would change my mother in some way. Alas, this was not to be, and as our teens advanced so did the outright violence and malevolent anger shown particularly to me, but my brother didn't get away scot free either.

I had three beautiful sons. My mother's comments were barely congratulatory: "You are making a rod for your own back if you keep picking up that child", shuddering as I breastfed as if she found the whole thing repugnant. Hours after giving birth to my much-wanted third son, she said, "Oh dear, you must be so disappointed, I suppose I shall have to wait for someone else to give me my granddaughter".

When my first husband and I went through a divorce, I was left with three very young children, a mortgage and only a part-time job. My mother, on examining the inside of my fridge, on one of her rare visits, told me that I was a lazy slut and that I should never have had children as I was an unfit mother. My response should have been along the lines of, "That's rich!", but as the cowed little thing I was, I said nothing.

I brought my boys up with ultimate and unconditional love, they came first in my life for the following fifteen years, until they were all living independent, happy, (hopefully) well-adjusted lives. I have a fantastic relationship with each of them, interesting and interested young men that they are.

I have a relationship with my own mother now. It is not the relationship that I would have wanted…the time for that passed many years ago. I do believe that therapy and guidance have certainly helped me over the years. I am very happily married to a wonderful younger man with whom, if circumstances had been different, I would love to have had a child and do it all over again. I don't think I would change a single thing that I did before except perhaps incorporate a few tricks I have learned along my way to becoming a crone. Most of all that potential child, like my actual children, would know above all else that they were loved in a way I never experienced myself.

Your Past is Not Your Future

I always knew I wanted children. My husband says he thinks I was born broody. Unfortunately, I miscarried with my first pregnancy, which really hit me hard. I remember thinking I would give anything in the world just to have my babies (I was carrying twins). I did feel some pressure to try again quickly as my mum had terminal cancer and I really wanted her to meet her grandchild. But I waited.

About a year later I was ready, and I got pregnant very quickly. I was apprehensive, but very excited. We paid for additional scans for reassurance. I took a course in hypnobirthing and really wanted a natural, calm birth. In my case this was not to be. After a traumatic labour I had to have an emergency caesarean. This did not impact on the amount of love I felt for my son from the second he was born. I felt that I had loved strongly in my life, but nothing could prepare me for the depth of feeling I had for this tiny, helpless creature. Sometimes I find it difficult to be a mum and still be me, but I am always working to find a balance.

As a young child I loved my granny. Then, when I was around ten, my mum cut off all contact with her. That was when I found out my granny was an alcoholic. In fact, we had come from a few generations of mothers being alcoholics. My mother had been neglected terribly as a child. Even as a baby she would be left alone for whole days at a time. She was physically abused and mentally tortured. My mum grew up feeling completely unloved by her own mother. This was something that haunted her for her entire life. She suffered terribly with depression for many years, but she always made us feel loved. She held strong values and morals and passed these down a generation. She was compassionate and thoughtful and, very importantly, she made us laugh.

When I think back to what it was like growing up, our house was always noisy, due to either passionate debate or laughter. My mum was a cuddler, this is one thing that I miss the most since my mum passed away a couple of months ago. She would wrap her arms around me and I felt safe and loved. There were things in life that she could not cope with, but she always tried her best. She was determined to break the chain and be a good mum, and she was.

I spent the majority of my teenage years being annoyed with my mum. But she was always the person I wanted to call. I eventually came to see that she did a good job and really tried hard to encourage me to find a life that would make me happy. I will always remember her saying that all she wanted for me was for me to be happy.

When I first found out my mum had cancer I was absolutely gutted. I thought, very selfishly, about the fact that I was going to lose my mum and how impossible it was to imagine her not being around. Your mother represents where you come from. You may not want to replicate this completely with your children, but she is your core, a major part of who you are. I cannot comprehend how my mum must have felt not having this. Not having that person to turn to and to nurture her. This thought has been amplified by having my own child. I look back on my mum's upbringing, whilst looking at my baby, and cannot understand how you could mistreat a child. I think about how it must feel as a child to love a person unconditionally, who does not show any love in return. I often think about a song my mum wrote. In it she explains that her past was horrible and she could not change that, but this did not define her life. What did define her life was how much love she gave her children and in turn how much love we show our children. She has broken the chain, she achieved her lifetime's ambition. What a worthwhile dream it was.

A Different Path

I found I was pregnant at nineteen, unexpectedly. I was in a bad relationship with a man sixteen years my senior. I had no family around me to speak of, and a handful of friends. I was depressed throughout the pregnancy, and the birth was an exhausting four-day endurance.

Shortly after my daughter was born was the last time I saw my own mother. I had postnatal depression. I'd had a horrific time and was craving support. We met for tea and she held my daughter briefly. But she only talked of herself. I decided then that she could give nothing to my life and that there was no room in her heart for my child either.

My first year with my daughter was a roller-coaster of leaving my partner and finding myself living on my own for the first time, as well as going to work. I felt I was becoming my mother. And so, when my daughter was about fourteen months old, I decided that wasn't going to happen. I stopped working, I starting taking an interest in my child, and learned how to cook and eat properly. I learned how to play for the for the first time in my life. I met my now-husband shortly after this, he took on my daughter like she was his. We began to plan another child, and are blessed with another daughter. My husband adopted my first child and I felt a huge relief that she had a chance at a normal family.

My mother is narcissistic. She became depressed before my father left. I was the youngest of three, she neglected us horrifically. I have begun to recognise how important food is in my life due to the lack of it when I was a child. Happy memories were only there from visiting a few relatives, my aunty and my granny stick out most in maternal memories. I liked how being with them made me feel. Food was a big part of that interaction, there would always be lovely food and a dining table set out beautifully. Like in books. They were not very physically affectionate, but I see them as my role models.

After social care removed us from my mother when I was ten, she stopped contact. I tried to keep it up and to understand why she speaks to my brothers, but I realised that you don't have to like your parents just because they're your parents. At times I have been bitter that I don't have what normal people have: a mother to help you plan your wedding, cuddle you when things go wrong, go shopping with, be proud of you, be on the end of the phone. I was never going to have this from my mother, even if we had stayed in touch. I feel like someone who lost their mother when they were a tiny child.

My children are older now and I am enjoying them more. I spent their formative years stressing over money, work, identity, fitting in and doing things 'right'. Now I work in children's services myself, and I can see I did a good job; I wasn't a bad mum and my children are turning out okay. I have broken a cycle before it began. Sometimes I hear my mother in the things that I say, but I am aware of it and stamp it out quickly.

I couldn't enjoy being a parent until I let go. And it took me nearly eight years to do that. We have a lot of family time. I make a monumental effort to educate my children on life and living, I help them be independent by teaching them how to cook and clean. We talk about why people behave in certain ways and how to cope with situations, we use cognitive methods to keep a positive spin on things. It's hard work and we don't achieve it every day. But I feel I am on the right track.

I see my role as a grandparent as a very high honour. I hope I am around long enough to give guidance and knowledge to those generations and the same passion to them to pass onto their children and grandchildren.

Without Her

The transitions of birth and death are closely related, and sometimes they cross over. One woman describes being beside her mother as she died, not knowing that she herself was already pregnant with the next generation. She wonders if her mother, on some level, would have experienced the existence of this new life.

Women who have lost their mothers before, or whilst, being pregnant, voice a heart-breaking sadness that their mothers and grandchildren will never get to meet one another. The grandmother, mother, child triptych will not exist for them in the flesh. The loss is a gaping hole that cannot be filled. Their grief is profound and may take different forms throughout pregnancy, birth and their child's development.

Yet simultaneously these women recognise that something of their mother lives on in their children: biologically, behaviourally, maybe something of their spirit. The physical absence of their mother does not stem the flow of maternal love: maternal lineage exists independently, irrespective of the women in it being alive.

I was fascinated by how these stories differ from those with fractures of trauma. Whereas the trauma appears to split, divert and dam up the river, the death of a mother does not in itself do anything to stop the flow. For some of these women there is even more awareness and appreciation of this love in their mother's absence, and a determination to keep it flowing on to the next generation.

I Miss Her

Being a mum has exceeded all expectations and I absolutely love it. My very special partner and I have two girls who are delicious and hilarious, with never a dull moment. They are two-and a-half and five months old at the time of writing this.

My first pregnancy was perfect and I had a magic time. The birth, however, was physically hellish: thirty-six hours of posterior agony. She arrived in hospital, in the end, with the help of forceps. I adored her instantly, but my body was destroyed.

The second time around I didn't enjoy the pregnancy so much, however the birth was powerful, fast and furious. It was only four hours of, well... agony, but this time at home with an amazing crew. A few hours later, after getting over the initial shock of what had just happened, I fell completely in love with my second daughter.

The girls have the most incredible father – a total dude – and together, to me, the four of us feel like a dream team. I hope I am a good mum. I really try my very hardest to be, but they are easy to parent. I am completely overwhelmed with how perfect my girls are, even when they wake at 4:30 in the morning with no intention of returning to sleep! I often look at them all and pinch myself with just how lucky I am, I love our every day.

My mother was a brilliant woman and I wish every single day that she was here with us. She was British and met my dad, a New Zealander, whilst on a world trip. They had four children, three girls and a boy. She was an artist, fantastic printmaker, illustrator, painter and sculptor. She died in 2006 of a heart attack, completely out of the blue, aged fifty-seven. I had just had an amazing weekend with her the week before she died. Her death was shocking and absolutely devastating.

She raised us to be pretty self-sufficient, as she was. I craved her attention and at times just wanted her to be more a 'mum' than this wonderfully independent woman and friend. There was a time when I got angry at her and I really had a go at her for various things like sending us to boarding school: it was awful. I carried the guilt of that day for years, but not now. Since becoming a mother myself, I realise you're not necessarily going to get everything right. Being able to forgive and love yourself is so important in allowing others, like our own daughters, to make their own mistakes.

Mum was a strong woman and against all adversity she laughed and carried on. I miss her so much, sometimes the loss feels unbearable.

I am, without a doubt, morphing into my mother. The way I am as a mother has a direct correlation to the way I was raised by my own mother. The way she was with us was absolutely affected by the way her parents were with her.

I am acutely aware of this and therefore love how much I am like my mum. But I also do some things very differently to the way she did. I want to have the same closeness I had with my mother with my daughters. Because Mum was so much fun to be around and we all adored her so much, going to boarding school was actually quite painful. Because of that I would never send my children away to school. In fact, I have to be careful not to smother them with love, as I wished to be smothered by my own mum. I want my daughters to, above all else, love and nurture themselves. In doing so, I hope they will naturally love and nurture others and through these relationships will have a rich and wonderful life.

She Filled My Cup With Love

My partner and I met over ten years ago. I knew pretty early on that I wanted to have a family with him, but we were still young. We married and after a miscarriage later that year, we fell pregnant with our first son the following year. Three years later, we were blessed with the arrival of another son and I feel truly completed by my gorgeous boys. I relished every bit of my pregnancies, loved the challenge and transformation of birth and now that I have truly surrendered to motherhood (it took a while!) I feel happier and more contented than ever before.

Despite not having my mum around, I am supported by very loving and caring family and friends. I have many female figures in my life that, whilst they could never replace my mother, give me great guidance and inspiration.

My mother died very suddenly from a brain haemorrhage when I was thirteen. Being an only child, my dad and I sort of raised each other until I left home at eighteen. Sadly, he never really got over the loss and passed away a few years later. Of course, I deeply miss both my parents, and in becoming a mother myself, there are endless times where I wish I could just pick up the phone and chat to my mum. However, something about having my own family has also been very healing, like the completion of a process. In many ways, I don't feel that loss as acutely as I once did.

There are definitely elements of my own upbringing that have influenced my parenting. I have a strong sense of being deeply loved as a child and I imagine that my 'cup' was overflowing with this love, so that when tragedy struck I was far better equipped to deal with it. Consequently, I feel passionately that the more love I can give to my children, the more resources they will have to call upon in the future.

Knowing that my mum lives on in my boys is an amazing thought for me. I feel so sad that they won't know their granny in person, but she is very present in our lives: in pictures, stories, and through other family members. My current life is so full and happy, and I truly feel I have her to thank for that in some way, perhaps through the experiences she gave me in our short thirteen years together. Also, in the different outlook I was given by losing her at that time in my life. Without that experience I don't think I would be the person, or mother, that I am today.

New Beginnings

I've always known I wanted to be a mother, but at one point I wondered if I would ever become one. I'm now pregnant but before this pregnancy I lost a baby. Although it was very early on, it has shaped my experience this second time round. In some ways I can't wait for the baby to be born. At other times it terrifies me. I would love to know now that everything will be okay, so that I can finally allow myself to get really excited and start imagining more of what motherhood may be like. But maybe the uncertainty can also be a gift, a reminder to be with my unborn child in the here and now, without thinking too much about what the future will hold. It is an opportunity to feel my body changing and making space for this new life. A reminder that I'm already a mother.

It's amazing how feeling so ill during the first trimester can also make you feel so happy: knowing that the nausea, tiredness, spotty face and breast tenderness are signs that all is well in there. Seeing the baby on the scan, with its tiny heart beating was one of the most touching experiences of my life. It is just incredible to think that my body can do this, that it can harbour and nurture a tiny cluster of cells into becoming a little human being with arms, legs, organs and a mind of its own. And to think that within this experience lies the promise of so much more.

I lost my mother eleven years ago. Losing her changed my life, and changed me. Growing up she was always there, a constant presence, mostly loving, warm and caring, but also controlling and frustrating at times. For some years it was just the two of us. Looking back, I think everything she did, she did for me, to make me happy. We did so many things together: laughed, cuddled, baked...

One of my earliest memories of her is when we once both woke up in the early hours one morning and couldn't go back to sleep. We decided to get up and bake some cinnamon rolls. I was about five at the time, I was so excited.

During my teenage years my mum and I went through a difficult time. I became stronger willed and my mum's controlling side came out more. We fought a lot. I smashed plates.

When I went off to university we became really close again. And then she got cancer. Seeing my strong, loving mum become thin, weak and tired was heartbreaking. Amazingly, she still continued giving, always doing everything she could for my siblings and for me when I was home visiting.

I had planned to move back home for a year after finishing university, but sadly we only got ten days together before she was taken from us. Continuing without her has been a journey in itself. Most of the time it's okay these days, but sometimes it's bumpier than I feel prepared for.

One of my biggest regrets is that my mum will never get to meet my children. Being pregnant has really brought home the loss of her in a new way. It's easy to imagine what she would have been like as a grandmother. Warm, caring, loving, always wanting to give as much as she possibly could.

I imagine we would have had many conversations about ways of making nature an important part of my children's lives, and taken them out to explore nature together. When I was growing up, I didn't appreciate how much richness my own experiences with nature gave me, but now I am keen to make this a big part of my children's lives too.

Even if my mother is no longer with us in person, her spirit, and her mothering of me continue to live on within me and will undoubtedly also be a part of my children's lives.

Learning from the Negatives

I became a mum at thirty-nine, after wrestling with every angle of family issues through my twenties and thirties. Then came a realisation that it could be what I wanted it to be, if I just relaxed into it. After miscarrying the first time round I had no expectations of having a live child. This meant I made the most of the relationship with the new child growing inside me: if our time together was going to possibly be only this, then let's enjoy it. I laughed lots, went to the pictures, enjoyed life and my food with the idea that this should be enjoyed for what it is. My wee companion was just inside me, that's all, and not on the outside.

I did not enjoy joining the mother club and felt suspicious of the evangelical high-on-life super-mums. I found I gravitated to individuals that were incredible parents despite having definite gripes about the job.

My greatest challenge is to stay soft and compromise and adapt. My rewards were totally unexpected and most welcome, "Love you mum!" before she sleeps never feels earned by me when I know I have not been perfect in any way during the day. But that's still there even if I don't try. I get my unconditional love from a source I never expected.

Memories come to me without warning and I have learnt to invite them and live with them. There is no timeline, they just illuminate themselves at whim. They are all childhood or young adult memories, as my mum died when I was twenty-one. Smell is most important: she smoked, and the spit wash with a tissue on your face was always a mixture of lipstick and nicotine. The sound of flip-flops on calloused heels with the washing basket on the hip while she walked down the garden path puffing furiously. She was a bony woman with freckled skin, tight over her breastbone. She didn't look made for hugs, which is a pity because I'm sure she needed them. I wish there were better memories of her, but the ones that hold are about anger coming from her about her situation in life.

I placed my bets on my mother-in-law's female line when thinking about having children. On her side the women live long, have resilience and are adaptable and strong. She is the same age as my mother and shares common history: both were illegitimate, but her parents stayed together and loved each other, while my mother was put up for adoption and had a life with money but no security.

I now have a better understanding of my mother, as I share the same experiences she had through her life. I am grateful for the negatives, they have given me great insight into how I approach motherhood. I know that my child cannot destroy me, but I can destroy her. I take that into account every day, it is a good lesson.

The Same Love

We had waited a few years after we married to try for a baby; as with everything in my life it was all meticulously planned and analysed. A few weeks after we started trying, my mum, who had had breast cancer twice in the previous fifteen years, felt unwell and was admitted to hospital. She had a huge unexpected growth in her liver and we were told she was dying. Twelve days later, she died. I was devastated. Five days after that, I found out I was pregnant.

I had some counselling to help me to deal with the emotional mayhem that followed. I wanted to know how to grieve and feel as despairing as I did, but also to feel the joy I had about my pregnancy and future baby. I felt very connected to my baby as he grew. He had been in the same room as my mum when she died, unknown to us all, a little piece of a happier future inside me. I hoped that she had somehow known he was there. When he was born I felt her loss very acutely. I've felt lost a lot in the ten months he's been here.

I'm an only child and my mum and I were extremely close. I remember as a child taking a piece of her old blouse with me to school sprayed with her perfume to keep her close during the day. She was always supportive, on my side, looking out for me. In return I wanted to please her: doing well at school and getting into university. It wasn't that we didn't ever argue, we did of course, but I always knew that whatever I did it was never so bad that she wouldn't love me anymore. That was a constant. I think we knew each other better than anyone else, even my dad, until I had gone through university and sort of needed to distance myself and grow up. I think this was painful for her, but she didn't tell me so, she wanted me to be happy. We sort of came back together in my mid- and late-twenties in a new way. With the same huge love for one another but as separate entities now.

I think that the unusual transition I had from having a mother to being a mother has made me look more deeply at the way I parent and love my little boy. I really feel that the love I have for him is the same love my mum poured into me. That the way she loved me directly influences how I love him and how I show my love to him. I find myself calling him the same affectionate names she used to call me without thinking. I sometimes feel like she's with me at 3am. I really mourn his loss of a wonderful grandmother and get very frustrated when people complain about their mums, but I know I would have been exactly the same had she been here!

I don't do everything in the same way my mum would have done. I hope I can be a bit more relaxed with him in terms of achievements and goals and allow him to fully become himself, whoever that is.

The Love of
Other Mothers

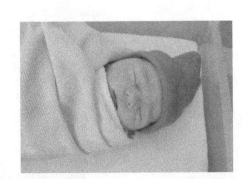

Our maternal inheritance does not come just from our mother. It reaches back to our grandmother, great-grandmother and far, far beyond. It also comes through our aunts and great-aunts, and through the 'other mothers' in our lives: mothers-in-law, adopted parents, foster parents, childminders, family friends, teachers, neighbours… Maybe more of an ocean, than a river, of maternal love.

These women connect not just with the love of their mothers, but with the love of other important women in their lives. They see how this matriarchal inheritance shores them up with love and wisdom. As they become mothers themselves, they gain strength from this great ocean of women and pass this on to their own children. As in the African proverb, "It takes a village to raise a child," they recognise that we need the support and influence of many people to have the inner strength to raise our children.

Would She See It The Same Way?

My baby should be born in about three weeks. We decided to try for a baby, and it happened shortly after. So far, the transition to be a future mother has been very natural. The body takes over, and while I have had to find some peace with the fact that it does not function the way I used to know, it helps me to be open, 'go with the flow' and take things more slowly, a process I am still reminded to carry on doing. And it has done me good, too, thus I am thankful for the baby to have forced me a bit in this direction. The pregnancy so far has been lovely. The first three months were tough, but I had a very supportive partner who literally cared for me every single day, cooking for us, feeding me, nurturing me when I needed it. I am very thankful and love him very much for this. I knew he would be a great caregiver, and I cannot imagine him being any different with our child.

I recall my mother doing things for me. But I do not recall cuddles with her. I cannot say whether there were none, or whether I just cannot remember. A stronger maternal figure in my life was my grandmother, she cared for me when my parents were at work. I have many warm memories of her – cooking, spoiling me with nice words and food that I still wish for now. There was a big break in our lives at the age of nine, due to me moving countries. I believe it shaped my life quite a bit. When we settled, my family carried on as before, but my grandmother was not there anymore to care for the children. I think now that this was a rather sad aspect that created a lot of distance between me and my parents. I was by myself a lot, not only physically, but also emotionally.

So far, my mother has been very anxious about the pregnancy, which has not supported our relationship. I have felt pushed and overwhelmed by all the information and desires that were hers, not mine. I have had to learn to set my boundaries, which I believe was quite a shock for her.

I think there are several big issues for my mother to explore for herself and I can imagine my pregnancy has triggered a lot of emotions for her. I do not know how my mother will be as a grandmother. I know she is looking forward to it. I also know she was very happy for me to become pregnant. Perhaps she had some very good memories of her pregnancy with me? My parents always told me how happy they were when they found out.

I do not want to think too much about the possibilities of how things might turn out. We will cross that bridge when we get there. Perhaps it might bring us closer. Perhaps not. I wish for my mother to be more at peace with herself, and to have time and head-space to sort out her worries. I would not want her relationship to her grandchild to be the same unaware and unreflective one that it has been with her and me.

Women of Strength

I never expected to be a mother, I just never imagined myself as one.

When I discovered I was pregnant it was a surprise entry onto a path I'd not thought about walking. I was an only child with very little contact with extended family and had never been around babies. The first baby I ever held was a little boy born about two months before a midwife was telling me to pick up my own daughter from the birthing pool. Nothing could have prepared me for the rush of emotions, the love, happiness, and worry about the responsibility that was now mine.

The early months were a steep learning curve, and a battle to breastfeed left me feeling like I wasn't cut out for this motherhood thing. Over time, though, with support and encouragement from friends, family and online communities, I have settled into this unexpected role.

I don't think any mother ever escapes worrying about her child, but it is worth every worry, every tear, every sleepless night to watch with pride the person growing and developing before my eyes. Five years into this unplanned journey I am so thankful to have someone that calls me Mummy.

I grew up in a matriarchal family, with my mother as a single mother supported by her widowed mother. Both of them were greatly influenced by my great-grandmother, a strong figure who raised twelve children in 1920s and 1930s Ireland. They weren't women to verbalise love and emotions, but you knew it was there. My grandmother was like a second parent in my childhood, and losing her to dementia was a big blow. They both made their expectations clear, but neither ever used physical discipline and rarely used harsh words. This has greatly influenced my own parenting style for my daughter as a fifth generation, firstborn female in a family shaped by women of strength. The three generations before me have faced many struggles in their lives but have shone through to the next generation as loving mothers.

During my teenage years the relationship between my mother and I became strained and my move to university was an important change. Distance between us helped us to communicate in a much better way. Now, however, we still live far apart and the distance makes me sadder than before. My mother and daughter cannot have the sort of relationship that my grandmother and I enjoyed, and since my mother-in-law died before my daughter arrived, she does not have someone to enjoy that with.

I have followed my mother in not using physical discipline and I try not to use harsh words. I remember my experience of my mother's mental illness though, as I, too, have struggles with this. I know that I want to change things for my daughter in how she experiences what I may be going through. My daughter may not have the experience of a grandmother, but I know that, thanks to the women before me, we can hopefully enjoy what they did too.

Biological Mother, Adopted Daughter

I thought going into motherhood that I had it figured out. I got pregnant much quicker than I had expected to and felt extremely lucky. But I developed a pregnancy-related illness called obstetric cholestasis which meant lots of hospital trips and many tests, through all of which the only person there for every appointment was my (adopted) mum.

The birth itself was induced early and I felt I lost all the control and understanding I initially had. Quite honestly, I was no longer prepared. The rocky pregnancy and birth shook my foundation, and I remember staring at my amazing little girl and not even remembering how to put a nappy on! Mum, of course, saved the day. The first few weeks she stayed with me and my husband, and was an enormous help as he went straight back to work. She kept me hydrated, fed and reassured through all the new mum worries.

At a few days old my daughter became unresponsive and so we rushed back to hospital where I was a blubbering, unhelpful mess, and my super-nurse-mum held me up. I began to become scared of the outside world after this, and became very isolated. It was Mum again who found me help and support.

My parents adopted me as a baby, and I have very fond memories of early childhood. My mum was strict but fair and always had my best interests at heart. We often clash heads about parenting styles, but we are very close, and I love her with my whole heart. I simply could not be without her.

My biological mother was not present in my life until my mid-teens, when by chance I located her online. At first it was lovely for both of us to find this mystery person that the world says we should be naturally close to, but that soon faded when the reality of trying to build a relationship around our lives needed to take place.

We are no longer in contact as she wanted to be my 'mother' and a 'grandmother' to my daughter, when I simply felt that was not her place. She had not brought me up through my awful teenage years, dealt with tantrums, cared for me when I was sick. So the role of mum and grandmother was the place of my (adopted) mum.

I am in no doubt that the way I was mothered has shaped the way I parent my own baby. I have held onto the importance of good manners, respect, and made it my job, just as my mum did, to help my daughter explore the world and its experiences as much as possible. But I also find myself suddenly using phrases that my mum used with me, even after promising myself I never would.

Being grown up, and a parent now myself, I have a real respect for what my mum did. She opened her arms and heart to another woman's child and stepped up to the role with enormous bravery and strength. She is the person I see as my mum, as grandmother to my daughter, and I really hope that I can show my daughter as much strength and love as she has showed me.

I've Only Just Sat Down!

I thought a lot about mothering a toddler; toddlers more than babies made me broody. Having my baby in my arms changed all that. I was smitten. My partner and I had sought couple counselling before deciding to have a child. Owing to complications in our early childhoods we knew things may be extra challenging for us. Our therapist suggested that if we wanted a child we should go ahead, saying that because of our insight and concern it boded well for us as parents. We were successful straight away. It was a bit of a shock, but I was so delighted. On the way back from the hospital, after a long and difficult birth, the world looked different to me as in a happy, hazy dream.

My transition to motherhood was intense but also wonderful. Initially my mother offered support when she could, but my partner took a very long time to adjust and struggled to support us as much as I expected. Over the coming months I became increasingly aware of feminist concerns and the ways in which our society falls short in caring for our children and their carers.

"I've only just sat down," my mum used to holler at my father as he came through the door at 6pm each evening. This repeated angry sentence stays with me until this day, and I think speaks volumes about being a mother in our society. Mum loves the sea. As a young child I remember a playful, creative, spontaneous mother, passionate about her children. She was caring but could get very cross. She stayed at home to raise us until school age. We were priority.

My mother suffered postnatal depression for a short time after I was born.

I was her first child. She was twenty-four and a midwife, her friends helped deliver me! My father played an important part in my life, especially at this time. This may explain my strong paternal bond. He speaks about a challenging conversation with my maternal grandmother who wanted to look after me instead, just as her mother (my great-grandmother) did with my mum. My maternal grandmother became an important figure in my life, especially as I got older and I would stay at her house regularly. She enjoys dancing, gardening and cycling, like me. She can suffer from anxiety, as do my mother and I. My relationship with my mother became volatile as I became older. On reflection I see just how complex my maternal line of relationships is.

My mother desperately wanted to support me during my early months transitioning to becoming a mum. She was aware that the start in life I had due to her mental health, may trigger in me too. I had a very intense experience in those days but was fortunate to get through it without becoming seriously unwell. Mum reliably came to support me one day a week throughout that first year, despite having a lot going on at the time in her career. This brought us closer together than it had done in years.

However, as time went on relational challenges returned. My mother retrained as a child psychotherapist. I'm very inspired and speak proudly of her, but crikey, I feel daunted by such an ambitious role-model!

My parenting is a blend of what I've learned independently and what I liked about my parents' way of doing things of which there are many: being present, listening, playfulness, creativity and exploring the outdoors. Of course, it's often hard to control our reactions and it pains me when I repeat negative traits that I experienced growing up.

I can see some maternal familial patterns weakening, having started a family later in life than my mother and grandmothers, and also because my first born is a son. Hopefully the personal work my mother and I do helps strengthen all our relationships.

Mothering is vital, physically and mentally demanding work, and it's okay to just sit down.

Breaking the Cycle

My first child was born on Christmas Day and every time I hear the Christmas song 'Little Donkey', I think of our treacherous drive on icy roads to hospital whilst I was in labour. My son was delivered by a female doctor in a hijab and a midwife wearing tinsel antlers, and the visual image of these two women tugging my baby out of me is one that I will remember for the rest of my life.

Looking back, I realise that the whole thing was a huge shock. Although I had wanted a child of my own for many years (my son was an IVF miracle, after several failed pregnancies) I was utterly unprepared for the reality of having a small baby that I was fully responsible for. I spent the first few months inhabiting a world that was both euphoric and full of anxiety. I have a second child now, a daughter, and what has amazed me the most is the lack of anxiety, and how easy and natural the transition to being a mother of two has been.

My mother brought me up by herself, after my father left when I was three. At that time (the early 1970s) very few families had just one parent. I remember her from my childhood as a strong, independent and professional woman who returned to her teaching career when I was just six weeks old. I partly admired her for this, but also partly hated her. However, the big plus of the choices she made was that I got to spend a lot of time with my childminder 'Aunty Brigid' and her large Irish family. I fitted in easily, becoming, in effect, her sixth child; I received the attention and bustle of daily family life that I craved. When Brigid died eight years ago, I felt as if I had lost my mother.

As I became a teenager, things changed a little. My mother and I began to do more things together, like going to the theatre and exploring our nearest city. But it was also the time that her expectations of me increased. She tells me now that she is proud of me, but if I'm honest I'm never completely convinced!

My adult relationship with my mother is, I think, fairly healthy. We are able to talk about most (but, importantly, not all) things. She has stepped back from me since I had my own children, and I wonder if this is because she thinks I don't need to be mothered any more. She loves the idea of grandchildren, yet struggles with the reality. It feels, as it did in my own childhood, as if something is missing. I guess history is repeating itself. It fuels my determination to make sure that I break that cycle, or at least alter it slightly, and to ensure that my children are loved and hugged and touched by me on a daily basis. However, I also hope that they will take some of my mother's values and pass them on to their own children.

Maternal Figures

I didn't know what to expect with my first child or how the baby would be born. There was a level of shame, so I would never ask. The little bit I knew was from NHS information, but even that wasn't enough. My first was a caesarean, my second a natural birth.

My first child didn't move around much, but I didn't have any experience to compare it too. I didn't talk much to my mother or mother-in-law about it, I was too shy. But my mother-in-law was very supportive, she encouraged me to rest and eat well.

Having my first child changed me, I was happier, as I had no family of my own close by. Having him was a great connection as he was my family, I had someone to look after. My grandmother was also in the UK and she was supportive and helped me to look after him.

I was my mother's second child. My older brother had died soon after being born. My mum was very caring and worried a lot about me. If ever I was poorly she would really look after me. Even as I got older my mum wouldn't eat without me. My aunties are all maternal figures, although they are all in Pakistan.

My mum would shout to discipline me; she never hit me but my younger siblings would get smacked. My mum had two daughters who died at the age of six, both were physically disabled and my mum looked after them as much as she could. In Pakistan she didn't get any support. Losing three children and then having me in the UK on my own made her really worry about me. Even now if I don't call her for a couple of days she will call and ask if everything is okay. My other siblings can still get jealous.

I now understand why my mum worried so much. I often worry about my own children, and when I do, I will call her. She has a good relationship with my boys, they speak on Skype. Language is a barrier and they ask her to speak in English. I think my mum tried hard, she told me some good things and taught me not to get involved with other people's arguments. I teach my children about respecting adults, and to treat them with love and kindness as my mum did with me.

I have to be stricter here in the UK, as in Pakistan we had all our family and community in the same place. We all believed and encouraged the same things, religiously and culturally. In the UK I have to constantly remind my children about their identity and the things that matter to us as a family and community.

Healing through Motherhood

Becoming a mother opens a door. As a new life enters the world, relationships are rearranged, and fresh roles formed around this new being. Mothers become grandmothers, siblings become aunts and uncles. The open door allows for all sorts of possibilities, including the expansion of feelings of love and the potential for healing.

Some women experience a deep healing in the act of becoming a mother. Perhaps it heals something within their bodies, or within their pasts. Maybe they see the world through new, more understanding eyes. And as their own mothers become grandmothers, there is the opportunity to form an entirely new entity: a maternal triptych where grandmother, mother and child are all related, all connected.

Motherhood can transform problematic, cold, or ambivalent relationships, with oneself and others, into something new. The love and warmth associated with motherhood can permeate not just the bond between new mother and child, but multiple relationships and experiences.

This is not a given. Motherhood is not a cure-all, but it does contain within it the potential for change.

Healing Experience

I had a very happy transition into motherhood, almost euphoric. My first pregnancy was brilliant, I've never been so happy in my body. The second was a lot harder, but both births were empowering experiences. I struggled a lot more with two children. I felt just as much love for my second baby, but didn't feel so euphoric. I felt a lot more isolated.

I struggled with body image after pregnancy, but also felt a lot less self-absorbed. It made me tackle issues from childhood, as I was fearful not to pass them on to my children. It made me really question the parenting I had received, good and bad.

Becoming a mother has been a very healing experience. More fulfilling than anything I had ever done before, but also the hardest and most frustrating. Moments of pure joy followed by your patience pushed to its limits. The biggest challenges have been things like having to stand back and let my daughter struggle with things on her own. Its biggest rewards have included watching the relationship blossom and strengthen between my children.

Mostly I have good memories of my mother when I was a child, but our relationship also included long periods of absence. I remember her being the main person in my life up to the age of three, I remember her doing loving and fun things. Then, for quite a few years, I only remember my dad, as he had taken me to live with him. I was meant to see her as well, as we lived close. But he was dominant and aggressive, making it very hard. Now as I parent, I know I would never allow someone to do what my dad did to my mum. But I don't feel any blame or anger towards her about what happened.

There were periods that I did live with her which I have very happy memories of – stories, cuddles and so on. As I got older, I realised how she struggled with worrying about things. She can be overly pessimistic and was not very good at standing up for herself.

As a teenager she was pretty hands-off, in that she trusted me to make my own decisions and supported them. On reflection, more involvement from her would have been good, but she was always accessible.

My mum is deeply loyal and supportive of all her children. She is very moral and lots of fun. A friend as well as a mother.

I have a very good relationship with my mum. We are very close, and she is always there for me. I am, however, quite aware of how bad she feels about the fact that I was with my dad and not her as a child. Since having children myself, I realise how horrible the situation would have been for her. We have talked about it, but I know it could be explored more.

I do think how I was mothered affects the way I mother, however I have worked hard to choose the aspects I feel are more positive than others. Overall, I hope that I'm passing on some of the amazing qualities that my mother possessed, and also I feel I am stronger in myself.

My mum has a great relationship with my kids, I only wish they got to see more of her.

In the Midst of a Trans-Generational Healing Crisis

I have two children. The birth of my second was problematic. She was without oxygen for seven minutes – clinically dead – a little, grey, lifeless body. She received a hypothermia treatment, with 16% chances of complete recovery. I felt dead from within but simultaneously felt as if millions of mothers, ancestors, cells, were screaming, crying and mourning through me at the same time. It was unbearable. I remember wishing I could be in a forest to scream it out.

During the first night, I went to stand over her for a very long time. I eventually found peace within and I told her that I would respect her choice. She could live if she wanted, she could die if she wanted, but if she was to not recover from the damage left to her brain and body, I asked her to die. The choice was hers. I never planned to say those words, they came from I don't know where, with peace and strength, but I don't think I have fully recovered from having pronounced them. There is still sometimes a little nagging feeling of guilt as if I had expressed that night a selfish part of myself I had always hoped I didn't have: shouldn't a mother's love be more unconditional than that? Anyway, she chose to live. We were able to take her into our arms for the first time seven days later – oh joy!

My mother and I have a good relationship, I love her, and she loves me. We have our darkness and light, and our relationship comes with its fair share of better and worse moments. My mother's childhood wasn't easy nor very happy. She is a very strong and determined person consequently, and she wasn't going to perpetuate the patterns of her predecessors. This, too, came with its fair share of positives and negatives. Our relationship really started to flourish during my early- to mid-twenties. Since then, our relationship has evolved into one where we are both conscious and willing to share, discuss, say, question and receive. Although our lived experience isn't the same, some traits and unconscious beliefs are funnily similar, probably taking their roots in the same genealogical events. We are both working together, consciously, to clear some rubbish, cobwebs, skeletons, ghosts and wounds from the past and the present. We have agreed to use our mother-daughter link to evolve together and individually as much as we can. We are more or less always in the middle of a trans-generational healing crisis… but I think we are doing alright.

I am more than happy to give a lot of space to the relationship between my mother and my children. She lives in Canada, we live in England, and consequently we don't see each other very often. So, when we do, we do. As far as I am concerned, life is short, grandparents are not there forever and you only have one shot at it. She is very present when she is with them, and they are too. I love to see them together, and, at the same time, I find it healthy for my children to learn to deal intimately with more people than just us, their parents. Everybody reacts to situations differently, it's good to try something different and my mother provides them with something completely different than I do. If it makes everybody happy, why not? I try to do the same with their paternal grandmother. There, again, the relationship is completely different, following her personality.

Helping to Rebuild Family Ties

In our twenties a few friends offered to be a sperm donor for me and my wife. As we got older and more serious only one person was still up for it, which made the decision easy! We did the insemination at home, just me and my wife which was exactly what we wanted.

Being pregnant was amazing, but also really tough, as I continued to work long hours. Giving birth was incredible and I managed it drug-free. The first few weeks were really hard. A week after the birth I went back into hospital with mastitis and was there for four days. Luckily my baby was able to stay with me. Being off work and spending time with our baby is wonderful. It is helping to rebuild family ties and I feel very at peace staring into her eyes all day.

We weren't a close family when I was younger. My mum and dad separated when I was fifteen, after mum had an affair. I moved out with my mum. I think my mum suffered with depression. She never spoke about it, but I found some medication in the cabinet. Looking back, I'm pretty sure she was depressed when she was with my dad. She drank a lot of gin through this time and I'd often find her passed out on the sofa.

Mum let me do whatever I wanted once we'd moved out because she was so grateful for my understanding and for staying with her. My sister was more of a parental figure for me and would check on me and make sure I was eating and looking after myself. I enjoyed the independence. Now my mum has remarried, she is very happy and drinks less.

It's lovely watching her with my daughter, it's so nice having someone who wants to smile and stare at her for as long as I do.

The mum I know now is very different to the one I had when I was fifteen. I plan to encourage our children to follow their dreams and passions. I want there to be open discussion around many topics so that they feel they can come to us with anything.

I'm sure there will be many lessons I will learn. As we grow, we tend to become more like our parents, so a challenge for me is to be mindful of this. I will always make time to listen to our children, however busy I am. In the future I would like to foster and fill our house with children and dogs and revel in the chaos!

Changed for the Better

I got married at nineteen and left my family to live in a different country that I knew nothing about. I went to Finland with my husband and got pregnant in the first year. I knew that having a child was a big responsibility and hard work. I felt I had trained with my mother because I am the oldest girl of her children and helped her a lot with my sisters.

My first pregnancy went well without any problems. I got a lot of support from everyone I knew and when it was time for the baby to come, my mother-in-law came and helped with the baby. She stayed for three months and was very helpful.

The first thing I did after I had my baby and understood what it means to be a mum, was to call my mum and apologise for everything I had done in the past and ask for her forgiveness.

My mother is very loving and caring. She is a strong woman. She looked after me and five other children while my father was working in a different country to support us. My mum is generally very kind, but she is strict when necessary. Our relationship changed after I grew up and we understood each other better.

My relationship with my mum changed for the better after I had my own children. The way I was mothered had a big effect on the way I mother my own children. I am quite happy with it, but I have had to change some things as the time and country are different.

She has a very good relationship with my children. They really love her and are always asking to visit. When we do visit her, she tells me not to worry about anything related to my children and she takes full care of them. She tells me to look after myself, visit my old friends and take time for myself. My children are happy to see that, and happy that she takes good care of them.

A Mother Reborn

My transition into motherhood was very emotional. I felt quite isolated and stressed. I was eighteen years old and had little support. My daughter's birth was very difficult, as were my other two with my sons. I suffered with post-natal depression, but during my recovery I found my identity as a woman, a mother, reborn, and embraced my new role. I felt empowered and am now thriving as a mother of three. I am so proud to be attachment parenting with children aged five, four and sixteen months. I never lack the motivation to be the best role model I can be.

My childhood was very disciplined, not full of good memories. It's something I've had to come to terms with over the years. I don't remember my mother being loving, affectionate and close. She raised five of us single-handedly, so I was responsible for caring for my brothers and sisters from a very young age when she went to work. I have learnt not to 'put' on my children or put pressure on them: just let them be children.

My relationship with my mother has always been quite strained, but over the last years, since having children, it has gone from strength to strength. She has been supportive at times and she is a doting nanny. She increasingly spends more time with them, and I appreciate the bond she has made with them. I try to surround my children with love, security and positive relationships, something I never had.

Motherhood is not what I expected, it's not the stress, mess and toddler tantrums I thought it would be. It's fun, enchanting and every day I learn something new.

So Happy with My Little Family

As a child imagining the future, I never thought that I would have a loving partner, or a family of my own.

I started personal therapy in my twenties, and this was a transformative process for me. It healed childhood pain, and was a kind of re-parenting for me. It was in my late twenties, when I was in my first serious relationship, that I began to imagine I could have a family of my own.

At twenty-nine I was pregnant. It was a happy accident and my partner and I were excited about this new stage in our lives. During the pregnancy I had high blood pressure and was in and out of hospital, I was induced to speed up my labour but at nine centimetres dilated, my baby was deemed to be in distress and was delivered by C-section. She was healthy, and I recovered well.

Motherhood has been a wonderful journey. I breastfed my first for twenty months, had four months break and now I'm pregnant with my second, who we conceived on the day we stopped using contraception. He's due in January and I am going to try for a natural birth. I am so happy with my little family.

I was born two months premature, and was in an incubator for a time. My own mother had postnatal depression and struggled to bond with me. I was worried that I might feel the same. But I was able to breastfeed in the recovery room, and my loving bond was strong and wonderful from the beginning. I'm not a perfect mother, but I am warm and unconditionally loving. My daughter is confident, and I hope she can dream herself a positive future.

I think for my mother being a grandmother has been a way to heal her relationship with me, and also something that has come more naturally to her than being a mummy. She's never been one to talk about feelings, but I know she is proud of her bond with my daughter.

I work with families now, and I'm so glad that there is more of a culture of talking about feelings and asking for help now, though there could be more support available. With the right support I think my relationship with my mother would have been different, and there has been a missed opportunity there. My daughter is only two years old, but she cares for her toys as if they are her babies, carries them, and loves them dearly. I know she'd make a wonderful mother if that was the path for her.

Motherhood Brought us Together Again

Motherhood for me began a couple of years before my eldest child was born. I saw a glimpse of the complex journey ahead. I felt an urge to get my house in order. To refine my life, to chuck out the unhelpful, old clichés about myself. Pregnancy and labour were a rite of passage. I celebrate the mother that was born into the world that night.

There are lots of things that I love about my mother. She is ditzy, strong, determined, funny, silly, strategic, a tigress. I love her.

But somehow the mother of my childhood got muddled, distorted, lost and misunderstood over time. We got into a twenty-year battle of miscommunication. But finally, we resolved it. We found each other. Motherhood brought us together again. It reopened the channels of communication between us.

I don't know exactly what has changed, but the boiling, seething rage that used to lurk just beneath the surface of our relationship seems to have dissipated. I feel a huge sense of love and respect flows between us now.

I love being a mother, my life is full of love. I find the hardest thing is to find the space for myself, but I get the feeling that that comes with practice.

Today a stranger on the bus said to me "you have your mother's face. You are born in the shadow of your mother. I can see her in your eyes. She is your strength, it is through you she speaks to the world." This is the truth.

Nine years on from the birth of my daughter, the seed of me sown so many years before in my mother's womb is emerging from the earth. My life before motherhood lies below me, rooted in my mother. Now I have emerged into the world with my daughter close to my heart, as I was once to my mother. And in the gentle sunlight of love our future is unfurling, opening to absorb its warmth. So that even a total stranger can see my mother in my face.

Exploring Your Maternal Lineage

Exercises and Activities

As you can see from the stories in this book and your own experiences, our maternal lineage is a rich tapestry. Its beauty, detail and complexity can greatly inform our lives if we take time to gently examine its different threads.

I believe that all women, not just mothers, can gain from this experience. Those with children and grandchildren may find they can explore the threads that trail both onwards to their descendants and backwards to the generations that precede them.

There are many ways to embark on this exploration and everyone will have an approach that is as unique as their lineage. If you would like to follow the process we used during our Mother in the Mother workshops, that led to the creation of this book, here are some simple steps to guide you:

1) Individual exploration

This may feel like a very personal piece of work that you want to undertake alone.

Many women, on learning of the project, wrote their stories online in three recommended sections, following a series of prompts (see end of chapter for details).

You can download a form to write your story at **https:// one-story.co.uk/resources/**

These sections were:

+ You and your Child/ren
+ Your Mother and You
+ Your Mother, You, Your Child/ren

Begin by collecting together some photos of the women in your maternal line, including yourself and any children you have. Lay these out together and look at the similarities and differences. Look into the eyes of each person. Consider how they might be feeling.

Then either go to the paper doll exercise detailed below, or straight to writing your story in line with the stories contained in this book. It's a good idea to set aside at least an hour for the writing. Firstly, write your responses to the prompts free-flow without stopping, focusing on your immediate thoughts and feelings. Then go back, look at the photos again and read what you have written. Creating a title for your story can help to focus your central theme.

Finally, edit your writing to convey what you most want to say. What are the key themes or emotions you want to capture? We recommend approximately 250 words for each section to help keep your writing focussed.

2) Group sessions

You may want to undertake the exploration with others. All of the workshops I ran began with finding or forming a group of women.

You may be lucky enough to already be connected to such a group – formally or informally. If so, you could suggest this as an activity for your group, to take place over several meetings. It's a very personal, and often sensitive, topic, so don't expect everyone to want to get involved.

If you don't have a group, you can go about forming one, perhaps with friends, local parents or community members. Put up a notice at your school, playgroup or nursery, or on social media, online forums and noticeboards. I suggest limiting the group to six people, including yourself, to give plenty of time and space for everyone to share. Find a nice cosy venue – someone's kitchen or front room will often do the trick – and you can rotate this to share the hosting. Hot drinks and cake go a long way to creating a nourishing atmosphere!

Children

For those with small children, consider how this will work. I find that non-crawling babies are fairly easy to accommodate in a group, if the mum knows she is supported to be there. However, if the entire group have toddlers, this is a different matter! When running workshops, I always stated in advance that the sessions were designed to be nourishing, reflective spaces for mothers, and ideally women would attend child-free. That said, we would

often have one or two children who needed to be there and always found a way to work around this, providing activities for the younger ones or taking it in turn to look after them. Most important is that the mothers are able to be there, and that lack of childcare isn't a barrier.

Setting intent and creating trust

Before you start working together it is really useful to set the intent for the group and make sure that everyone is on the same page. To build trust between the group, it is helpful to state an agreement of confidentiality so that things shared within the space remain there. It's also good to request that any comments or feedback remain positive and respectful, so that no one feels criticised.

It helps if it is a closed group, committed to working together, so that you

don't have people dropping in and out. Decide how long the sessions will be – we worked for two to three hours – and how many times you will meet. I suggest three to six sessions depending on how many of the activities (listed below) you would like to do.

I would also state at the start that the work can be quite revealing and sometimes upsetting. Encourage participants to make sure that they have suitable support outside of the group, especially if they are dealing with traumatic issues. You may want to set up a private online group or shared chat so that you can share thoughts and feelings between the sessions.

Sharing

It helps if one person is able to 'hold' the group, making sure that everyone has time to share. This is not always an easy role. If no one fancies this position, you can use a timer to help people keep track of how long they have. I find that women are often highly attuned to knowing when to share and when to listen. However, sometimes it can help to have some boundaries in place to keep things on track.

I would always start a session by asking each woman to give her name, the ages of any children she has, and to say why she was interested in taking part. From here, the family stories will start to unravel.

Activity: Paper Dolls

This was a favourite exercise that we included in every workshop. It's something many women remember doing in their childhoods, and can provide a great activity for any children in attendance.

You will need sheets of different coloured A4 paper or thin card, scissors and pens. Fold the card into three in a zig zag shape. Draw a figure on the front piece of card and, importantly, make sure that the arms reach the sides of the card.

The figures can be as simple or as complicated as you like. With the paper still folded into three, cut out the figure, making sure not to cut through the place where the arms reach the sides. Open the paper out, and – hopefully – you will have three figures, holding hands. This is your maternal lineage: from left to right the figures represent you, your mother, and your maternal grandmother. Write these titles onto each figure then write beneath each title three words to describe that person.

Where women have not known their maternal grandmother, they have written things they may have learnt about her through their mother or other people who  knew her. If women did not know their mother they focused on the person with the most significant maternal role in their life.

This activity does not have to represent a biological family. It can be an adopted or foster family, or anything else that represents your maternal lineage to you. Decorate or embellish the dolls as you choose.

Activity: Paper Dolls Discussion

Working around the group, share the words you have written onto the paper dolls and how they make you feel. Talk about what the experience of finding the words was like. It may be interesting to reflect if there are similarities or patterns in the words chosen for each doll.

Many women struggle to find words for the doll representing themselves. Some women may have only one word on each of the dolls, whereas others might cover them in adjectives. If there are feelings of anger, shame, hurt or fear, some women will find it hard to write these down. Others will love putting pen to paper. In the very first workshop I ran, one woman chopped all of the heads off her dolls! It's not about getting it 'right', but the experience of doing the exercise, and how the participant feels.

Make sure that everyone who wants to has the chance to share their words with the group. As reflections are shared, themes and connections will often be made between the women in the group. This is the beginning of weaving your own group tapestry of collected stories. If you have somewhere you can peg all the dolls to hang up together this creates a useful visual point of reference.

Activity: Photo Reflection

Ask each woman to bring approximately ten family photos of the important women in their family, as well as of themselves and their children. Where possible, ask women to bring printed copies. If you have a reasonably large table, invite each woman to spread her photos out and take some time to look at them as a group. Ask each woman to talk through who is who, and to reflect on what it was like finding the images and seeing them laid out together. Again, look for similarities, patterns and differences between the way each woman shares her stories.

Activity: Maternal Lineage Poster

You will need card (A3 or larger), scissors, glue and coloured pens. Invite each woman to arrange the photos she has gathered onto a piece of card, in whatever pattern makes most sense to her – linear, circular, scattered, etc.

Then, draw lines, words and pathways between the images to illustrate connections, fractures, love, complexities, and anything else you would like to visualise. You may want to use string or coloured thread to show the links between the images. If you remember anecdotes relating to specific women, or the relationships between them, you can add these alongside the photos. Spend as much time as you like on this activity and embellish the poster as much as you want.

By the end of this activity, each woman will have created a unique poster of her maternal lineage. You could display them together to create a collective representation of your group's maternal history.

Extended Activity: Visual Narratives

If you would like to develop this piece of work further, you can each create a handmade book using images and words. As you work you may find that there is a story you want to tell about the women in your life and the relationships between them. Your book can be as simple as A3 pages folded together and tied with ribbon, or as complex as you would like to make it.

There are many great resources, in print and online, for creating handmade books. (We used *Making Handmade Books* by Alisa Golden. Lark, 2011.)

There are several other ways to create visual narratives: depending on your time, skills and resources. You could use the images and words gathered through the paper dolls and poster activities as inspiration to stitch a patchwork of maternal memories, make a line of bunting, or make a short film. For some examples of visual narrative projects visit my website at: **https://one-story.co.uk/one-story-projects/**

Whatever you create, ensure that you have time to share it within the group, giving all participants the chance to reflect on and discuss their stories. You could also arrange a mini exhibition to share your paper dolls, maternal posters and visual narratives with friends and family.

Writing Prompts

You and Your Child/ren

Describe your transition into motherhood

Prompts: Did you have clear expectations beforehand? What was your conception experience, did you go through IVF? How were your pregnancy/s and birth/s. If you adopted, fostered or became a step mum what was your transition to motherhood like? How were the first weeks and months, did you feel supported? Did your sense of identity change? What have been some of the greatest challenges and rewards of being a mother?

Your Mother and You

Describe your mother

Prompts: Was your biological mother present or absent in your life? Did you have other maternal figures – relatives, foster parents, adoptive parents, friends? Describe your mother as you experienced her as a child. Do you remember her physicality, her closeness to or distance from you, her style of parenting, the way she showed love, the way she disciplined you? Were there any times you were particularly close or in conflict? Did your relationship change as you became a teenager or in relation to other life events?

Your Mother, You, Your Child/ren

Describe your adult relationship with your mother

Prompts: Did your relationship with your mother change when you had children of your own? What do you think now about the way you were mothered? Do you feel the way you were mothered has affected the way you mother your children? Are there things you do consciously or unconsciously that are either different from or similar to the way you were brought up? What is your mother's relationship with your children? If you are a grandmother, how does your relationship with your grandchildren differ from that with your own children? Describe its particular joys and challenges.

Afterword – reflections on participation

Ella

There have been huge changes in my relationship with my mother since I started this project, we seem to have resolved something between us. It has been wonderful to have a creative outlet and to reflect on how motherhood has positively impacted on my life and mended my relation-  ship with my own mother. Thank you for your creativity in devising, and tenacity in accomplishing, such a wonderful, life-enriching project.

Charlotte

"Stories have to be told or they die, and when they die, we can't remember who we are or why we're here."

Sue Monk Kidd, *The Life of Bees*

My mother sits on a blunt edge of me. I am not sure when I started wanting so much from the relationship and I can hear how ridiculous that sounds. Of course I wanted a lot. Our mothers are literally the centre of our universe;

the universe of the feminine, the universe of self. My mother. My world. She made mistakes, sure. Some big mistakes. But isn't she allowed to stumble and trip? She loved me, but somehow I just didn't feel it to be enough and I have never really recovered from this longing.

For the whole of my adult life, I have been trying to unpick the complexities of my feelings towards my 'not quite good enough' mother. When I expand the idea of my mother, my world, as a concept, I can see how I have interacted in the world from the central place of how things were between my mother and I.

So, when I heard about Pippa's exploration into this vast landscape, I grabbed it with both hands. I was part of a group of women who, with the gentle holding of Pippa, explored the difficult relationships with our mothers. It was raw, brittle, complex and yet rich, moving, and enlightening.

We tentatively shared parts of our experience, but perhaps the most powerful aspect for me was the space it provided to be quietly reflective and to consider how this was now shaping my own challenges and triggers in my relationship with my children. There was a family constellation aspect to the movement of my feelings. I reflected on my grandmother's story and the impact this had on my mother and her relationship with her daughter, me, and the impact that was having of my own mothering. I considered what my mother had held from an historical ancestral point of view and wondered about what my children now hold in their 'field' by being part of this lineage... and how the whole experience speaks through my grandmother, my mother, myself and now my children.

All of this wondering, quiet reflection and creative work evoked a deep sense of perspective, compassion and curiosity in me. This was such a resting place, after so many years of anger, resentment and reaction. From this new understanding I was able to communicate differently in my relationship with my mother and also to appreciate the dynamic revealing itself in my relationship with my children. But most importantly I was able to start the soft conversation around forgiveness – for my mother, my children and myself. I made a quiet gentle commitment to end the suffering. I was forty-four years old when I took part in this project and this consideration was new.

Since the project, I have been able to offer my mother and myself a little more forgiveness. I am not an example of perfection, but I am embodying the 'good enough mother' and hopefully this is all my children need to grow up capable of taking part in the world in a meaningful way.

Joy

It took me a long time to write my story, but it was a very rewarding experience. It helped me move on from some painful memories and accept things I hadn't before. It helped me accept my mum's and my own imperfect parenting. It made me think more deeply about the relationship with my children and grandchildren. I feel closer to my daughter than I have for a number of years.

Silole

[Mother in the Mother] gave me an appreciation of the experience of my grandmother, my mother and how I am as a mother. I think it was an understanding of the influences of the times and circumstances when my grandmother and mother were parents. I've also appreciated how my grandmother affected my mother's mothering and how my mother's love towards me was such a gift and how it has enabled me to naturally feel very loving towards my children.

Amy

My mother and I were very close, however she passed away suddenly aged fifty-eight, and the years that followed bought a deep grief. Because it was so painful, I went to great lengths to avoid facing her death. Therefore, when I was asked to take part in Mother in the Mother, I was initially quite apprehensive. I had become a mother myself to two wonderful daughters and because of this I was also feeling her absence more than ever. However, I decided to participate.

We were a group of women who had all lost our mothers at various ages in our lives. It was incredibly powerful hearing each story, learning about each woman's perception of her relationship with her mother, their experience of becoming a mother themselves and the continued influences our mothers have on us still. Pippa held the group with wisdom and sensitivity, creating a safe space for each of us to comfortably share our story.

I decided, as part of the workshop, to make a short film about my mother.

It required me to spend days sorting through photos, going through her boxes of things, which I hadn't done for a very long time. I hadn't expected it to be as cathartic as it was. Since becoming a mother myself, I was suddenly finding myself looking deep into her face in each photograph, scrutinising her emotions, analysing how she held us four children and what was going on in the background. The process opened up a new way of relating to her as both a woman herself, and to her as my mother.

Mother in the Mother has had a continued influence on my life in three ways. First, I had felt very much a victim after my mother passed away. I rested in a place of injustice and felt her death was incredibly unfair. By taking part in this project I was given insight into the diversity of relationships between mothers and daughters through frank and candid storytelling. It allowed me to see how incredibly lucky I was to have the relationship I did, despite it being cut short.

At the same time, I started to accept that my relationship with Mum was not perfect, which I had immortalised it to be. This lead to my second wave of thinking: my mother had her own life challenges. At times I felt incredibly let down by her and angry. Mother in Mother gave me space to fully accept her, both as a woman and a mother, to fully appreciate the sacrifices she made and forgive her for decisions made. Forgiveness that I hope will one day also come from my own girls as they battle with my ways.

Finally, I savour in the lineage that has been passed to me by my mother from her mother and no doubt from hers before her. This appears most obviously in the way I express the love I have for my daughters. There is a deeply familiar and completely natural way we snuggle up, proving the affection and love I was shown by her.

I see huge value in Mother in the Mother and am incredibly grateful to Pippa for guiding me through this experience. We should all be offered the space to explore our lineage through storytelling, it's a powerful tool for understanding our memories, healing our relationships and accepting ourselves.

Emma

Writing my story was very therapeutic and empowering. The whole process has helped me to accept and appreciate all of my experiences more, from being mothered to being a mother myself. I have been able to let go of the guilt and be more proud of how I mother my child and how well my mother did. Overall this has helped me with my confidence and joy in being a mother.

Misty

I've felt nurtured by Mother in the Mother, both personally and professionally. During my pregnancy and my early motherhood journey, this project has been an important part of my life and has helped me reflect on my identity as a mother and to concentrate on what matters. Essentially, this project has been a catalyst for change in my life.

References

Ainsworth, Mary. *Patterns of Attachment – A Psychological Study of the Strange Situation*. Psychology Press. New York 2014. First published Lawrence Erlbaum 1978.

Apter, Terri. *Difficult Mothers*. Norton. USA 2013.

Aull Davies, Charlotte. *Reflexive Ethnography*. Routledge. Oxon 1998.

Baraitser, Lisa. *Maternal Encounters – The Ethics of Interruption*. Routledge. Sussex 2009.

Bowlby, John. *A Secure Base – clinical applications of attachment theory*. Routledge. London 1988.

Bowlby, John. *The Making and Breaking of Affectional Bonds*. Routledge. Oxon 1989. First published by Tavistock 1979.

Bright, Susan. *Home Truths – Photography and Motherhood*. Art Books Publishing. UK 2013.

Cixous, Helene and Clement, Catherine. *The Newly Born Woman*. Manchester University Press. Manchester 1987.

Cusk, Rachel. *A Life's Work*. Fourth Estate. Great Britain 2001.

Donaldson, Julia. *Paper Dolls*. Pan Macmillan. London 2012.

Ettinger, Bracha L. *The Matrixial Borderspace*. University of Minnesota Press. 2006.

Friday, Nancy. *My Mother, My Self*. Delacorte Press. USA 1977.

Gillies, Val. *Marginalised Mothers – Exploring working-class experiences of parenting*. Routledge. Oxon 2007.

Hays, Sharon. *The Cultural Contradictions of Motherhood*. Yale University Press. New Haven / London 1996.

Kitzinger, Sheila. *Becoming a Grandmother, a Life Transition*. Simon & Schuster. London 1997.

Lawler, Steph. *Mothering the Self – mothers, daughters, subjects*. Routledge. London / New York 2000.

Lareau, Annette. *Unequal Childhoods – Class, Race and Family Life*. University of California Press. 2011.

Northrup, Christiane. *Women's Bodies, Women's Wisdom*. Piatkus. London 1995.

Northrup, Christiane. *Mother-Daughter Wisdom*. Piatkus. London 2005.

Odent, Michel. *The Scientification of Love*. Free Association Books. London 1999.

Perrier, Maud. *Developing the 'Right' Kind of Child: Younger and Older Mothers' Classed Moral Projects*.

Perrier, Maud. *No right time: the significance of reproductive timing for younger and older mothers' moralities* in The Sociological Review 2013. 69-87.

Perrier, Maud. *Middle-class Mothers' Moralities and 'Concerted Cultivation': Class Others, Ambivalence and Excess.* 655-670.

Phoenix, Ann, Woollett, Anne and Lloyd, Eva. Motherhood – Meanings, Practices and Ideologies. Sage Publications. London 1991.

Rose, Jacqueline. Mothers – An Essay on Love and Cruelty. Faber and Faber. London 2018.

Stadlen, Naomi. *What Mothers Do – especially when it looks like nothing.* Piatkus. Great Britain 2004.

Stadlen, Naomi. *How Mothers Love – and how relationships are born.* Piatkus. Great Britain 2011.

Reynolds, Tracey. *Caribbean Mothers – Identity and Experience in the UK.* Tufnell Press 2005.

Rich, Adrienne. Of Woman Born – Motherhood as Experience and Institution. Virago. London 1977.

Winnicott, Donald W. *The Child, the Family and The Outside World.* Penguin, London 1964.

The project was kindly supported by:

Mother in the Mother workshops took place with the following groups:

+ Platform 51
+ Mothers for Mothers
+ Bluebell Care
+ The Meriton School
+ Knowle West Children's Centre
+ Bristol Woman's Voice
+ Bannerman Road Community Academy

Thank you to:

Carolyn Hassan for believing in my work, it has made all the difference.

Bart Blazejewski for endless design reiterations and supporting this project from its outset.

The wise and wonderful core group of mums who helped to ignite this project at meet ups in 2012: Nina Stinchcombe, Karni Arieli, Refkah A'Court Mond, Catherine Waters, Misty Tunks and Sam Burkey.

My first readers: Sylvia Holliman for her encouragement, Claire Stewart for getting the introduction into shape, Alex Wardrop for waking up my brain cells and Rachel Clarke for her endless enthusiasm, brilliant editing and enlivening intelligence.

Lucy, Patrick and Leigh at Womancraft, I'm so glad to be publishing with you.

My family, friends and community for your endless support - you mean the world to me.

And most of all thank you to all the story contributors and project participants; this is your book.

About
the Author

Pippa is a socially engaged artist, writer and sculptor. Her work brings together over 24 years of training and working in the worlds of holistic health, body work, dance, creative writing, journalism, film, photography and sculpture.

Pippa has run participatory arts projects with a diverse range of communities since 2001. She facilitates the sharing of stories and the creation of 'visual narratives' at beautifully held workshops. Participants tell their story using a combination of media including textiles, book-making, creative writing and digital storytelling. Pippa is particularly interested in helping to give voice to the quiet, every-day stories that may otherwise be overlooked or forgotten. Where voices have been silenced, Pippa's practice helps them find a creative way to speak out.

A passionate feminist for as long as she can remember, Pippa specialises in working women, exploring issues including motherhood, grand-mother-hood, menarche, the female body and trauma. In her sculptural practice, Pippa investigates the ways in which our personal and collective stories are frequently embedded within our bodies. All of her work is grounded by an ongoing fascination with, and research into, the healing qualities of literature, myth, fairytale, storytelling, dream and archetype.

Pippa lives in Bristol and is a mother to two amazing daughters.

www.one-story.co.uk

(f) motherinthemother

(y) PippaOnestory

(o) pippaonestory

About
Womancraft

Womancraft Publishing was founded on the revolutionary vision that women and words can change the world. We act as midwife to transformational women's words that have the power to challenge, inspire, heal and speak to the silenced aspects of ourselves.

We believe that:

+ books are a fabulous way of transmitting powerful transformation,

+ values should be juicy actions, lived out,

+ ethical business is a key way to contribute to conscious change.

At the heart of our Womancraft philosophy is fairness and integrity. Creatives and women have always been underpaid. Not on our watch! We split royalties 50:50 with our authors. We work on a full circle model of giving and receiving: reaching backwards, supporting TreeSisters' reforestation projects, and forwards via Worldreader, providing books at no cost to education projects for girls and women.

We are proud that Womancraft is walking its talk and engaging so many women each year via our books and online. Join the revolution! Sign up to the mailing list at womancraftpublishing.com and find us on social media for exclusive offers:

(f) womancraftpublishing

(y) womancraftbooks

(o) womancraft_publishing

Also from Womancraft Publishing

Liberating Motherhood
Vanessa Olorenshaw ISBN 978-1-910559-192

If it is true that there have been waves of feminism, then mothers' rights are the flotsam left behind on the ocean surface of patriarchy. For all the talk of women's liberation, when it is predicated on liberation from motherhood, it is no liberation at all. Under twenty-first century capitalism, the bonds of motherhood are being replaced with binds to the market within wage slavery and ruthless individualism. Mothers are in bondage – and not in a 50 Shades way.

Liberating Motherhood discusses our bodies, our minds, our labour and our hearts, exploring issues from birth and breastfeeding to mental health, economics, politics, basic incomes and love and in doing so, broaches a conversation we've been avoiding for years: how do we value motherhood?

The Hero's Heart: A Coming of Age Circle for Boys (And the Mothers who Love them)
Melia Keeton-Digby ISBN 978-1910559-437

The Hero's Heart is a groundbreaking new approach to raising healthy, compassionate, and emotionally intact young men. Innovative and timely, this mother-son curriculum is an answer to what our boys need in order to thrive – rather than just survive – in the current culture of traditional masculinity.

With genuine encouragement and invaluable insight, Melia inspires mothers to create the intentional communities, character-shaping opportunities, and rite-of-passage experiences that adolescent boys crave.

The Heroines Club: A Mother-Daughter Empowerment Circle
Melia Keeton-Digby   ISBN 978-1910559-147

The Heroines Club offers nourishing guidance and a creative approach for mothers and daughters, aged 7+, to learn and grow together through the study of women's history. Each month focuses on a different heroine, featuring athletes, inventors, artists, and revolutionaries from around the world, including Frida Kahlo, Rosalind Franklin, Amelia Earhart, Anne Frank, Maya Angelou and Malala Yousafzai as strong role models for young girls to learn about, look up to, and be inspired by.

Offering thought-provoking discussion, powerful rituals, and engaging creative activities, The Heroines Club fortifies our daughters' self-esteem, invigorates mothers' spirits, and nourishes the mother-daughter relationship. In a culture that can make mothering daughters seem intimidating and isolating, it offers an antidote: a revolutionary model for empowering your daughter and strengthening your mother-daughter relationship.

Moods of Motherhood: the inner journey of mothering
Lucy H. Pearce   ISBN 978-1-910559-21-5

Moods of Motherhood charts the inner journey of motherhood, giving voice to the often nebulous, unspoken tumble of emotions that motherhood evokes: tenderness, frustration, joy, grief, anger, depression and love. Lucy H. Pearce explores the taboo subjects of maternal ambiguity, competitiveness, and the quest for perfection, offering support, acceptance, and hope to mothers everywhere. Though the story is hers, it could be yours.

This is a book full of Lucy's trademark searing honesty and raw emotions, which have brought such a global following of mothers to her work.

Signed copies of all titles available from
shop.womancraftpublishing.com

CPSIA information can be obtained
at www.ICGtesting.com
Printed in the USA
JSHW030030270123
36521JS00006B/336